Best Poems of 1970

Best Poems of 1970
Borestone Mountain Poetry Awards 1971

A Compilation of Original Poetry
Published in Magazines of the
English-Speaking World in 1970

**Twenty-third Annual Issue
Volume XXIII**

Pacific Books, Publishers, Palo Alto, California
1971

International Standard Book Number 0-87015-195-9.
Library of Congress Catalog Card Number 49-49262.
Printed and bound in the United States of America.

PACIFIC BOOKS, PUBLISHERS
P.O. Box 558, Palo Alto, California 94302

FOREWORD

Best Poems of 1970 presents a selection of poems first published in the year 1970. The selections are from magazines of the English-speaking world. The publications and issues from which these poems were selected are acknowledged in the "Contents." By the time the compilation is completed, there are some subsequent reprintings of the poems, which are recorded along with other recognitions under "Acknowledgments and Notes."

This is the twenty-third volume of yearly selections since the Borestone Mountain Poetry Awards literary trust was founded in 1947. There have been two variations in titles since the first volume, *Poetry Awards 1949.* The fifth volume included the full name of the literary trust, *Borestone Mountain Poetry Awards 1953,* to avoid confusion with other "awards." The eighth volume identified the year of the selections, *Best Poems of 1955,* with the subtitle, *Borestone Mountain Poetry Awards 1956,* which continued the sequence of earlier titles.

The few requirements established for the first volume have never been changed. A poem is eligible if it is the first printing and not over one hundred lines. Translations, unpublished poems, and reprints from other publications and books are not considered.

The editorial procedure has also been consistent throughout the twenty-three volumes. Some three hundred or more poems are selected by the reading staff each year. When the year's selections are complete, copies of the poems are sent to the judges with the names of the authors and periodicals deleted, as there is no intention of recognizing established names in preference to the newcomers, or distributing selections between periodicals and countries. The judges score their individual preferences and forward the results to the office of the Managing Editor, where a tabulation of the scores determines the final selections. The three highest scores are the winners of the year's awards. Thus, there can be more than one poem by the same poet and a number of poems entered from the same periodical.

"Coda Bestiarum" by Laurence Donovan received the first

award of $300. "Thoughts from Torcello" by John Smith won the second award of $200, and "Lost Soul" by James Kirkup received the third award of $100.

The editors gratefully acknowledge permission to reprint these selected poems from the magazines, publishers, and authors owning the copyrights.

THE EDITORS

LIONEL STEVENSON	HILDEGARDE FLANNER
Chairman	FRANCES MINTURN HOWARD
HOWARD SERGEANT	GEMMA D'AURIA
British Commonwealth	WADDELL AUSTIN
Magazines	*Managing Editor*
(except Canada)	

ACKNOWLEDGMENTS AND NOTES

"A Soul, Geologically" by Margaret Atwood, selected from the first printing in the spring 1970 issue of *Prism International*, is reprinted from *Procedures for Underground* by Margaret Atwood, by permission of Oxford University Press, Canadian branch, and Little, Brown and Company, Boston.

"Chipmunks" by Ben Belitt, originally selected from the winter 1970 issue of *The Southern Review*, was included in *Nowhere But Light: Poems 1964-1969* by Ben Belitt, published by the University of Chicago Press in 1970.

"Saul, Afterward, Riding East" by John Malcolm Brinnin originally appeared in *The New Yorker* and was included in *Skin Diving in the Virgins* by John Malcolm Brinnin, a Seymour Lawrence Book/Delacorte Press. The poem is reprinted by permission of the author, magazine, and publisher.

"On This Particular Morning" by Jerald Bullis is reprinted by permission from *The Hudson Review*, Vol. XXII, No. 4, winter 1969-70, copyright © 1970 by The Hudson Review, Inc.

"Haunting the Maneuvers" by James Dickey was copyrighted © 1969 by Minneapolis Star and Tribune Co., Inc. and reprinted from the January 1970 issue of *Harper's Magazine* by permission of the author.

"No, Madame, I Won't Take Anything from the Garden when I Move" by Sonya Dorman was copyrighted © 1970 by Saturday Review, Inc.

"The Wig" by Charles Edward Eaton will be included in his sixth volume, *Lives in Danger*, being prepared for publication.

"The Messenger" by Thom Gunn appeared in his new volume *Moly*, published by Faber and Faber Ltd., London.

"Black Squirrels and Albert Einstein," selected from *The New Republic*, is part of a book-length poem entitled *Maximum Security Ward* by Ramon Guthrie, copyrighted © 1970 by Ramon Guthrie, and is reprinted by permission of the author and the publishers, Farrar, Straus & Giroux, Inc.

"Crow's Theology" by Ted Hughes was selected from the

We also note that copyrights on poems appearing in this volume have been assigned by the magazines to the following authors of the poems: Charles Edward Eaton, Kenneth O. Hanson, Margaret Peterson, Adrien Stoutenburg, Phyllis Thompson, and Paul Zimmer.

CONTENTS

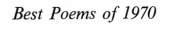

Best Poems of 1970

CODA BESTIARUM

1

The animals lie at the back of our eyes,
In all that narrows
Dying with us.
They perish continually
Like old flowers.

The brain is shaken in a wind of falling birds.

2

Adam, in naming them, named their sins:
Lionpride, bullrage, pigeonheart.
The corners closed like a vise upon them,
Earth assumed its tribal shapes,
And the high whirling wings
Plunged them
Into territories of their own keeping,
Spaces taloned and flagged.
They bled there one into another.

3

But only in Adam's bad eyes,
Only in him was their death,
Since they crept, swam, flew, mercury-pure
Through their corridors of tongueless love
Into simpler suns, into their own dark:

How they glide in their ways,
Roll featherwise in the loops of their lives,
Is our memory's wonder.

4

Still the lion's gold corolla
Medallions the leaves:
The quick and the slow, roe-

buck, ibex, turtle
Move round him there.
Still the plummeting whale,
The soaring giraffe,
The splayed porcupine
Stitch with the gull
The fabulous corners.

5

Time speaks best in these beasts
Who dream in the night and walk like themselves
       in the day
In the perfect shapes of their skin and fur
Scale feather and hide

They veil nothing their simplest mood
Says love says beware

Time speaks best in those who
Tiger, walk tiger
Giraffe, move giraffe
(In a long gaunt blur on the knobbled sky), who
Crow, croak and flap
And elephant, clump
(In great thickets of leather
Down delicate paths
To the prayerwheels and the waiting dark).

6

At the back of our eyes
Time turns into dark:
Panther and pard, all beasts of day
Lie now in our eyes:
The stilled ape and bear
Dream in their fur:
Here lie pigeon and wren:
Time turns into dark.

7

As the moon rises eyes of the animals rise from
    the forest into her light
Thief of the sun her turned forest deepens
Into what's burned by eyes
Living the dream of daybird and doe:
The undersides and despairs and drowned souls
    of the daybirds
Rouse in the moondrenched moss and rise
    to the moon
From black bushes, boles, the lifting branches
Through the dark to cathedral sky:

                                        there

Stareyes feed on the animal light
    and the widening night's
Born of its moon:

                        too soon
        day will come,
And the trumpeting sun, and the hunter arise:

                                                O

Let the lights flash in the silhouette world
Like fish speaking from water, let night
        look and look
From all of her eyes, and the turned forest guard
    the lair of the fox,
Slept turtle and doe, and turn ever slow:
        let the animals dream:
As the moon rises eyes of the animals rise from
    the forest into her light

LAURENCE DONOVAN

THOUGHTS FROM TORCELLO

A motorbus plies the tourists to the island:
Its name is holy. I am speaking of course
Of the island, not the boat, though that is irrelevant,
For it is not the object that matters but the fact
Of consecration. The island is uninhabited
Except for the figures who people the mosaics;
It is not known how they obtain their sustenance
Nor in what grave language they converse.
When visitors arrive they remain implacably silent.

They nest in the dome and arches of the church
In a mode of violent stillness. Outside, the vines,
Withering in autumn, let the grapes decay.
The grass is rank. The angel on the left
Has wings of black gold, the drapery of his shift
Seems the material substance of God; his scythe is deadly.
The winnowing of men by flood, by plague,
Disturbs the air no more than the faint haze
Wrought by the wings of gnats above the river.

Time has distributed the liberal flesh
Of the sometime human; the drowned and swollen bellies
Steamed in the prodigal energy of the sun
Five hundred shadowless years behind our backs.
But the beings in the dome, along the walls,
Keep their androgynous and hieratic shapes,
Or if one crumbles, splintered under the sharp,
The ineluctable eye of a pitiless God,
The fragments, hard as maize, lie where they fall.

The sprawling body of a dead man soon decays,
And though sometimes we weep is it not kind
That wind or waves or fire or the eating earth
Ravage that useless substance? The penance
Suffered by angels whether contrived or real
Is their endurance: to see beyond time

Illimitable years devoid of passion and love,
Knowing more sharply the cold condition of God
Whose algebraic nature scorns man's nescience.

No scouting traveller with his camera's jaws
Nibbles away those fifty thousand dead
But in appalling duplication hauls
Even the ghosts of these harsh artefacts
To flicker and writhe on a thousand vulgar walls
As the real Cherubim or Seraphim
Within the mouths of priest and chorister
Suffer perpetual despoliation
Their bright shapes dulled by the spittle of mankind.

Night draws a soiled sheet over the island's ribs;
The tourists have departed leaving a thin scarf
Of luminous petrol that blinks up at the sky
From the edge of the lagoon. In the smart hotel
Over the curious and unfamiliar drinks
Will one with no warning find his limbs go cold
And stare in terror out to that hallowed place
Not knowing who will shrive him of his sins:
God's holy vampire or the unregenerate dead?

JOHN SMITH

LOST SOUL

on a picture taken in childhood

No camera could ever catch again
This visage, old before its time,
Nor shutter the primeval rage
For solitude within
The absent social stance.

No tyrant power could exploit
That vulnerableness, no chemical expose
Its tender invisibility, nor print
The cat's wary nonchalance
In an affected poise.

Even when as here, in early childhood,
I defenceless stand, yet
Obscurely armoured in my undivided gaze—
A child alone, framed in a doorway:
A front of detestation in a scowl of pain.

*   *   *

Eyes lowering but straight,
Brow big, mouth still unschooled in smiles,
A little Taurus, about to butt his horns
Against a wrong already half-expected,
In a life already far too long.

The left fist clenched, in desperation,
As if for a battle he
Knew in advance not worth the fight.
(One blue eye, the right, is indeed
Already bruised and blackened.)

Baffled as an aborigine
Afraid to lose, with the taking
Of his likeness, an emergent soul:
A veiled yet penetrating gaze
Sunk in the sadness of primordial woe.

Wary of strangers' smiles
Suspicious of their ease, their looks,
Of hands bearing gifts, caresses;
Yet gulled with promises of beads,
Baubles, toys broken as soon as touched.

Knowing himself a fool, and like a primitive
In love with all that was frivolous, shining.
Unable to distinguish dream from life,
False from true, good from bad—
Perhaps not wishing to.

                    *   *   *

I knew it from the start,
And see now how much wiser I was then:
I am all there, the essence
Of the boy I cannot mask,
—That child the father

Of this man, that stocky dwarf
This delicate giant, that brave bull
This stricken deer, that dead David
This Jonathan—and this Goliath with the stone
Embedded in his brow.

He sees it now: the pattern and
The picture of a life, a death—
Something that did not have to be
But that a flash ordained as past and future
Somewhere round the age of three.

JAMES KIRKUP

THE DEATH OF AUNT ALICE

Aunt Alice's funeral was orderly,
each mourner correct, dressed in decent black,
not one relative berserk with an axe.
Poor Alice, where's your opera-ending?
For alive, you relished high catastrophe,
your bible, Page One of a newspaper.

You talked of typhoid when we sat to eat,
Fords on the M4, mangled, upside down,
just when we were going for a spin;
and, at London airport, as you waved us off,
how you fatigued us with 'metal fatigue,'
vague shapes of Boeings bubbling under seas.

Such disguises and such transformations!
Even trees were but factories for coffins,
rose bushes decoys to rip boys' eyes with thorns.
Sparrows became vampires, spiders had designs,
and your friends also grew SPECTACULAR,
none to bore you by dying naturally.

A. had both kidneys removed in error
at Guy's. 'And such a clever surgeon, too.'
B. one night, fell screaming down a liftshaft.
'Poor fellow, he never had a head for heights.'
C., so witty, so feminine—'Pity
she ended up in a concrete-mixer.'

But now, never again, Alice, will you utter
gory admonitions as some do oaths.
Disasters that lit your eyes will no more
unless, trembling up there, pale saints listen
to details of their bloody martyrdoms,
all their tall stories your eternity.

DANNIE ABSE

YOUR MAGAZINE HUSBAND

1

So finally after strolling along
through whistling constellations above your peaceful roof
three years,
      I saw you coming over the ether from the edge
      of your world, & remained silent.
      Through with striking
the dome of my brain & hoping for music,
I watched you approaching, like one of those floating-women
from fashion advertisements.
      Puffed-up, preoccupied with "art" & musing on
      postures, I remained silent
      as you sped by.
You passed by; without glancing sideways
at me, you passed with your billowing gown flouncing lightly
as your scintillating hair
      & your neck bare. Before distance sucked you in,
      before I could use my disapproving look,
      my temper flared
& sent hoops of hysteria bowling after you;
though you side-stepped the serious verbs & rolled with
my clubs of rhetoric.
      I hardly see you anymore, & when I do you have
      that "ah, Rimbaud—you'll grow out
      of him" look in your eyes.
Because I prefer silence: the spooks
of fallen heroes drift away in sunlight, even Rimbaud disperses
like curls of hashish on a draught.
      I have no sense of seasons these days, only
      crumpled balls of typing paper clenched in my fists:
      I miss your cups of instant-tea.

2

The slick pages of playboy magazine
are fingered by a breeze, each photograph scoops sunlight
& glossy nudes are silver glare.

I have lost the page of you, an artificial wind
flicks through the magazine of my mind;
at the door Something knocks.
You fumble with hesitation at the keyhole;
is it the obscenity of my love knocking to expose
itself?
But you're not here, you are somewhere Dark: you
are wandering the sky doing romantic things
with silk; you're dancing barefoot.
Clocks & the inevitable hourglass clearly show
time still to open the door,
Something waits.

Like a martyr, I rise up from my desk & shuffle
to the door thinking: if that's her knocking
I won't open.
& although we still lovetouch, we are separate
(normal logics for '69) so if you
can't open the door let me.
The brass lock turns & the door swings open;
wildlight of summer confuses us: & there's not
even a comment on such obvious symbols as doorways.

We stare at each other, & our own faces stare
back . . . we're not, after all
living "as one."
As the two sides of a magazine page are together
& with different numbers, we are blown along
together & separately
by dark personal winds.

ROBERT ADAMSON

A SOUL, GEOLOGICALLY

The longer we stay here the harder
it is for me to see you.

Your outline, skin
that marks you off
melts in this light

and from behind your face
the unknown areas appear:

hills yellow-pelted, dried earth
bubbles, or thrust up
steeply as knees

the sky a flat blue desert,

these spaces you fill
with their own emptiness.

Your shape wavers, glares
like heat above the road,

then you merge and extend:
you have gone,
in front of me there is a stone ridge.

Which of these forms
have you taken:

hill, tree clawed
to the rock, fallen rocks worn
and rounded by the wind

You are the wind,
you contain me

I walk in the white silences
of your mind, remembering

the way it is millions of years before
on the wide floor of the sea

while my eyes lift like continents
to the sun and erode slowly.

MARGARET ATWOOD

CHIPMUNKS

The sweet playfellow
is already aware:
taking a safe-cracker's stance
and turning the tumblers of air,
his paunch set down
like a reticule,
his ballerina's eyes
sootily bowed back
as for *Swan Lake,*
dancing the word for surprise
with his henna behind
and the tungsten crook
of his tail, his ears
like an adze
in the cinnamon and black
of his face's triangulations —

What draws love to its object,
unlike to like, impure to pure,
as my eyes to this?
The chipmunk, balancing the spike
of the acorn on prayed paws,
knowing the stations of the rodent,
finds kernel and meat
with his nose
like any other rat,
and packs the pulp home
with his jaws;
by wainscotting and sewer
a killer keeps his vigil
by a trap:

Love is content with that.

BEN BELITT

THROUGH OLD FARMHOUSE WINDOWS

Move your head and the view undulates.
Each pane is a watery lens. The apple trees

have rubber trunks. The road meanders more
than a road should. Even the modern house

on the next hill breathes a kind of passion.
From the attic's single, dollhouse window

we overlook a mirage of hay. Framed there,
the cattle stand, wrinkled as though by heat;

their spots wax and wane like shadow-play.
Our host, the farmer, sits teetering on his tractor.

Old glass can't distort him. He could be
any shape in his baggy overalls. Supper time

he clatters to the table, still trailing
mud and weeds and the day's irregular light.

ALLAN BLOCK

FAIR OF THE FIRE RING: LONG WINTER

in this old converted chicken house
the birds yet live, not tame fowl
    little sparling-sparrow
    creatures
    nest among the tin eaves
dig down with stretched feathers beneath
the green weather stripping
to keep out cold

snakes crawl under the rising floor
one, a summer past
left his skin behind, mice
root cotton out of chairs and all day
sleep, their tight round eyes

—come out at night
when the big animals, lights out
go to bed
stand on their heads, roll on chair fur
stick
their quick noses into our left hot drink
cups and stand
washing their fine whiskers

in the open now
they slide the painted curtains and
swing to the paper flowers
sent from Mexico—sit
wide aware faces
studying against flight, walk
on spread-toed feet over the wet milk platter
slick tails curled to their noses
  imagine
falling out from light
in their dark cave, when the stars come
low on the roof shining against the tin

like fire wheels, the little clowns
who are not like birds
that sleep all through dark, run
up and down the ferris wheel
climb walls most perpendicular, walk ledges
slide banisters and wade over the tea kettle
climb to our bed
in the still of where we've gone
to look at our faces

BESMILR BRIGHAM

SAUL, AFTERWARD, RIDING EAST

*And as he journeyed, he came near Damas-
cus: and suddenly there shined round about
him a light from heaven:/and he fell to the
earth, and heard a voice saying unto him, Saul,
Saul, why persecutest thou me?/And he said,
Who art thou, Lord? And the Lord said, I am
Jesus whom thou persecutest . . ./And he trem-
bling and astonished said, Lord, what wilt thou
have me to do? And the Lord said unto him,
Arise and go into the city, and it shall be told
thee what thou must do./And the men which
journeyed with him stood speechless, hearing a
voice but seeing no man. . . ./And immediately
there fell from his eyes as it had been scales:
and he received sight forthwith, and arose, and
was baptized.*
—The Acts of the Apostles, 9:3-18.

Still a bit dazed,
I study out the sequence—what
diverting cast of eye,
what random cocking of an ear,
could, with such fell abruptness,
bounce & so dishevel me? Was it
that fellow in the stinking fleece,
the black figs of his nipples bared,
who watched me drop like a drugged bee?
Those sullen beauties, broad as crabs,
bent to their lettuces & cress? The icy
chuckle of the spring
that rinsed their dragging purples
& vermillions? The two
blue mountains that were always there?

Today is yesterday; my hand,
all by itself, salutes
a door that closes,
or will close.

Hearing a voice (I did hear a voice)
but seeing no man (I saw no man)

I have listened to brass,
accepted any cupful, put on the eunuch's
fastening of silk, rolled over—
a good dog. No wonder
my old road is dark.

Still, the small flowers eat my dust.
Somehow, I wait upon the man I was—
of a commission & a large address,
of rectitude & ample documents.

I think my bones are melting. The reins
keep sliding from my hands.
I jog like a baby, loved.

Courage,
my bruises whisper: you are,
at worst, the subject of a rustic anecdote.
You would not come so far to disappear.
And yet,
this breath that takes my breath away . . .
What wilt thou, Lord, have me to do?

I feel the low sun pushing me to sleep.
Along the walls of these colossal shadows,
light like a rumor runs its fluted scale.
Nothing I see is visible.
Damascus! Damascus!

JOHN MALCOLM BRINNIN

GHOSTS

. . . ruined, futile writhing and unkillable defiance
—James Agee, *The Morning Watch*

Now the codger caretaker sleeps in the cemetery.
Dead to the world
            in the window of his hut
An empty jar of moonshine
Glows like the eye of a bobcat caught in headlights,
And what rises or falls now
            wildly
Accepts the power of simple expression that has been
From the beginning: it is time for ageing
Lovers to close their doors, windows, their curtains
Lock themselves together in the dark, and fly anywhere
Out of the harnessed land

On the wings of their nightmarish arms.
It is in this light, in which all forms are gigantic
And small enough to crawl in the marrow of bone,
That the snakes we killed in youth, hacked
To pieces with shovels, with scythes, chopped
In two with powerful mowers, flattened in shorn hayfields
Under tractor tires, or bruised with pitchfork tines
In the mellow gloom of barns,
            stuck on the points
Of wooden Arthurian swords, and displayed for the anguish
Of mothers, through screened-in back porches
            stir again

Again, and more than they did when alive.
Now something strangely sinuous may pass through the wall
Of timber
        move as naturally as the God of all
Things primitive into the vaporous lowlands, and tail-stand
On junked cars in the moon's white light.
In a yard where children dream in their tarpaulin wigwam,
A luminous kingsnake drifts out of honeysuckle, out of sweet-
smelling vines

                   and coils the handlebars of an unhoused tricycle:
On logging roads, on back-country county roads,
On the well-worn paths that cattle take to a thousand ponds

Copper heads are searching now for the whites of their bellies,
For the separate riven skins
That rise out of dust in the shapes they took when they died;
And on hillsides where men walk in darkness at noon
Ever conscious of Adam and Eden's
Thorn in the heel
                  the fungus of ancient timber
Moves: cracks: gives way,
As diamond backs rear up, up-
                     curl from the grave-
groping place like tongues, terrific as vampires
On the drive-in movie screen in the valley below—rear up

And fly with the grace of unknown beasts
To beat their wedge-heads on windows battened against them,
To crawl in ghostly skins, in leafy draintroughs
Of houses they never saw in their wicked, hidden lives—
Feeling for holes in the flesh
Of human dwellings
               for any way to get in, GET IN
In before dawn, before they crinkle like dust on a well-
house floor, in the cluttered corners of garages,
On staves in a kitchen woodbox beside the door,—
GET IN
          among the warm, the tremendous bared feet

They struck at mostly in vain, in their old sluggish days.

JERALD BULLIS

ON THIS PARTICULAR MORNING

I hear bravuras of birds. . . .
—Walt Whitman

1

Last night: March rain
Splatting, spits of brightness, thunder; the hills
Filling up like barrels with water
                                    runnels failing
To hold their own,—now this: I dress and pass out
Through my door into light.
                                    And the world is dowered by birds
On this particular morning, in this vaporous quiet
The red-bellied woodpeckers come to the feeders in pairs;
And the robins, those firstlings
Of spring wrangle toward me
                                    singing: warbling more good-
naturedly than musically—moving out
                                    down from the oak
Trees up along the ridge.
                                    Now the chickadee brings
Its three-note melody, and the white-breasted nut-
hatch trills as if
To the bewick riding upside-down on the suet feeder,
Swinging with it
                                    adding his mating call to the crazing
Grace of this quiet chorus,
                                    to the strophe, here!
And antistrophe out along the multiflora hedge
                                                        (where
White-crown and white-throat sparrows skirr and whirr)
—Where meadowlarks, now
And again!
                    take to the air with the flair of angelic
Quail.

2

      —In this loud stillness of the sun's slow
Rising
      now, like my long self's others, I
Would wingedly rise
Up wholly out of *it*
                  out of scythe-snath sickle
Whiffletree and clevis,
As my heart goes out to these like my whole self:
As overhead
The skein of Canada geese, that squall of honkers
Passing to some fake refuge in the far North,
Receives unknowingly my utmost blessing.
My desire in this particular light is the lost,
The forfeited grace of birds
                the incredibly clear
Call of the cardinal this morning, the unkillable strength
Of white-throat sparrows that in a week will journey
To the edge of the Arctic tundra.
              I would be, BE
By God with them, all of them,
              I think: or riding
The topmost limb of a timberline wind-gnarled pine,
In the dwelling-place of the last surviving buteos:
Learning the stormy élan of these jays—
              that are coming
Into focus like memory, like hell or high water,
Terrible as blood-
shed in the corner of my cornfield, coming out of nowhere
To strike, there!
Again, and there!
And more,
      more than anyone could handle in this life,—
Where they rip the stuffing out of the light-blinded owl.

JERALD BULLIS

FOR A YELLOW CAT AT MIDNIGHT

As though drifted inland
in some dark current of your own,
you settle against my side,
cumbrous as clay or a warm stone,
and I wake to find you there.

Why at night, small lion,
are you so much heavier than by day?
Only this afternoon
you slept, upside down, in a lap
already full of books and child,
and you were a tawny feather,
a fluff of sun.

Now pulled hard to the earth's center,
as though to a final place,
(lion, are we older by a night?)
we wait for sleep,
held fast by separate stars,
ponderous with what we do not know,
caught in a common dark.

JEAN BURDEN

TAKING LIGHT FROM EACH OTHER

We leave the mountains
framed in glass,
darkening in violet snow.
We turn from the lake
and the cold swans
and move toward each other
in a strange, familiar place.

Is it for this we came
so far,
fleeing entanglements,
only to be caught by these frail reeds?

Taking light from each other
we marry on a rented bed,
naked as children,
biting into the dimming day
as into a fruit.

Even as we love, the world
is constantly passing away.
(At home I would be winding my father's watch
against another day. How could he have died
younger than I am now?)

It is time to gather space into this shrunken room.
We let in lake and sky;
we clutch the mountain that endures,
fading as though for the last time,
and hold each other as we fall to darkness,
prescient of birth,
remembering what it is
to die.

JEAN BURDEN

NUNS AT BIRTH

This wing is quick with nuns. They flock and flutter,
Their habits whisper, sweeping the corridor.
The mildest human sound can make them scatter
With a sound like seed spilled on the immaculate floor.

They know about waste. They come with disinfectant,
Troubling the peonies bursting on my sill;
Their quick white hands can purge the most reluctant
Stain, and the sprouting germ, and the alien smell.

Old men have said—and my anxious, Baptist mother—
That purity is the fallow ground of love.
It is here in the sterile sheets and the smell of ether
And their bead-bright eyes. But what are they thinking of?

Or that Superior Mother about her labours:
What discipline could inform so bland a nod
When I shrieked and he shrieked and the bursting fibres
Gave him up to her quick white hands in blood?

Or the dove-grey novice now in her sterile plumage,
Who will go about birth, and about it: his hot greed
And my thickly weeping breast . . . what sort of *homage*
Brings her white hand fluttering to that bead,

Because it is that, my love! Her breath has quickened
At the noise of his pleasure in the immaculate air,
As if some glory sanctifies the fecund!
Well. Twenty centuries' lies are brought to bear

In her innocent misconception; the germ sprouting
In the cell, the chalk on the alien door, the hot
Salvation of witches, the profits and the prating—
We have not bought those lies. But we must have bought

Some lies. We are consumers, you and I.
And now this third, gums leech-fast at my breast,
Whom we shall wean to an epicure, and say:
Self-sacrifice is ingratitude, is waste;

And say: husk the kernel; feed at the fountains;
Seek sun in winter at the belly of the earth;
Go to the East for splendour, the North for mountains;
And always go to the nuns in time of birth.

JANET BURROWAY

AMARANTHUS

Here in this house
whose walls you painted and whose books are yours,
how shall I say what dies and what endures?

In this long wintering season, all about—
sudden between the pages of a book
indoors; or out
sifting among pine needles down through sand—
glitter the glass-bright and glass-fragile splinters.

Tender of these, I set myself to search,
collect, assemble, take them in my hands
with care, not losing one—and in some room,
some quiet room, furnished with crucible,
woodjack and blowing-rod,
make the flame take them, fuse them into flowers
blown to perfection as to permanence,
fashioned and wrought so there is nothing wanting,
nothing but color and life.

Frail hardy sterile stuff,
they will be rooted in a deeper loam,
and I shall keep them under a glass bell.

And then once more
I shall go down the sandy road, and look
at that great bush of small red living blossoms
insolent on the sight,
bearing their seeds of growth as of decay—
see it again, that day,
without resentment, and, it may be, even
again with pure delight.

CONSTANCE CARRIER

ACADEMIC PROBLEMS

From this eleventh-floor window they seem
To have a pattern, are perhaps simply
Analysable libidos slotted
Into predictable mod gear, making
Their urgently trivial way to coffee
Or sex (or the delicious combination
Of both) and I can discern from my chair
The neurotic redhead who will worry
Herself into the teaching profession,
The brilliant, conceited biochemist
Who will further develop Krebs's Cycle
And deceive his wife with a nymphomaniac
Lab assistant, educated with care
At St Ursula's convent. The scene disturbs
My sense of free-will. Higher still gazes God,
With his God's-eye view of both it and me;
My arm tightens around the Indian girl
In the next armchair as I fall in love.

The same sort of people live in Red China;
Lived, so the patient archeologist says,
In Babylon, Tenochtitlán, Lascaux.
'At different stages of class struggle,'
Added Karl (enclosed in the womb of the
British Museum) Marx. 'I see man's mind
As a surface crinkle on a massy ball
Of hidden strata binding a burning
Core,' whispered Freud, and every church crashed
At his feet with a roar of pain. If Christ replied,
I did not hear his words either in Greek,
Jacobean English, or the modern
Newspaper Dialect Version. Perhaps
We must consult Plato, Aquinas, Boehme,
Swedenborg, Goethe, and Rudolf Steiner?
Surely they detected a tiny signal
From Paradise on ultra-high frequency.

The historian warned me not to support
Either side in the war, and especially
Not the neutrals, the United Nations,
The Red bloc, the Black bloc, the Yellow bloc,
Or the Roman Catholic Church. He said
That I would be judged by History.
The moralist warned me never to be
Immoral. Except in exceptional
Circumstances. I rather liked him.

The philosopher wrote me a three-page
Mathematical formula. Mozart,
Without a word, went to the gramophone
And played me Concerto For Vaginal
Vibrator and Sonic Space-Counter. Fred
Zeitgeist demonstrated his invisible
Mobiles, created by diagonal streams
Of carbon monoxide in a polar field.
An art critic handed me an explication
Written in a language which closely
Resembled human speech. I did not thank him.

My wife, my mistress, and my six children
Make heavy demands on my conscience,
And now there is this Indian darling
Who teaches me the piano and wants me
To take Food Relief seriously, and support
Population control in Asia.
I am neither degenerate, wicked,
Nor insensitive. Nor am I
Albert Schweitzer, Buddha, Cleopatra,
Christopher Columbus, William Shakespeare,
Einstein, the Virgin Mary, Picasso.

DENNIS DAVISON

HAUNTING THE MANEUVERS

Prepared for death and unprepared
For war, there was Louisiana   there was Eisenhower a Lieutenant
Colonel and there was I
As an Invasion Force. The Defenders were attacking
And I was in the pinestraw
Advancing   inching through the aircraft of the Home
Force. Sacks of flour were bursting
All over the trees. Now if one of them damned things hits you in the head
It's gonna kill you just as sure as if
It was a real bomb
So watch it. Yes Sir. I was watching
It. One sack came tumbling after
Me no matter
What. Not in the head, though,
I thought thank God at least
Not dead.
But I was dead. The sergeant said go sit
Over there: you are the first man killed. It's KP for you
For the whole rest of the war. This war,
Anyway. Yes Sir. The Defenders had struck
The first blow: I was plastered. I thought why this
Is easy: there's not a drop
Of blood there's only death
White on me; I can live
Through.
I lived through in the Hell
Of latrine duty, but mostly on KP, on metal
Trays that dovetailed to each other, stacked by the ton in the field
Kitchens. I moved them all at one time
Or other, and the Defenders
Ate   ate and went back to killing
My buddies with blanks and bread. But when I slept on that well
Defended ground   the pinestraw stirred   each needle pointed up
Into the dark like a compass, and white   whiter

31

Than my skin, edible, human-eyed through the pines,
Issued a great mass
Laugh   a great lecture-laugh by the chaplain's one
Dirty joke, I rose
Over the unprepared boys   over the war
Games the war
Within a war   over the trucks with mystical signs
On them that said TANK   over World War One
Enfield rifles filled with dud rounds   self-rising
Through the branches   driven up like a small cloud
Of the enemy's food   at the same time bread
And bomb, swanned out like a diver, I came

From my death over both sleeping armies,
Over Eisenhower dreaming of invasion. Where are you,
My enemy? My body won't work any more
For you: I stare down like stars
Of yeast: you will have to catch me
And eat me. Where are you, invading
Friends? Who else is dead? O those who are in this
With me, I can see nothing
But what is coming   can say
Nothing but what the first-killed
Working hard all day for his vision
Of war says best: the age-old Why
In God's name Why
In Louisiana, Boys   O Why
In Hell are we doing this?

JAMES DICKEY

NO, MADAME, I WON'T TAKE ANYTHING FROM THE GARDEN WHEN I MOVE

Along the east wall built of rubble stone,
covered with ivy, the iris come up.
Green fans with a thrust rising from each
rhizome, unfolding on top: Desert Song,
Bronze Garland, Blue Lake, and Foxgrape.
From early May through June the wet tissues
fold in, crumpling, withered, like hands
finished with prayer.
In a moist corner behind the lilacs
I leave Monkshood for that woman
who doesn't know sour grass is good salad.

June. On the slope behind the house
under the dogwood's whiskered green berries
drifts of daylilies open from sweet green pea-
like pods, delicious boiled and buttered.
Out come daily orange flowers with tickling pepper
spots in their throats. I take the wilted
blossoms to simmer in my soups
while down below
thrives the Monkshood I leave for that woman
who'll lie in the sun and let weeds grow.

False Dragonhead, with serrated green edges,
rampages through bluebell and Veronica.
In August, when mildew's on the phlox and even
wild bees are weary, its raspberry-lavenders
blaze up the kitchen side where I make
a last dandelion salad before going, and I
smile at the secret
heights of Monkshood behind the lilac boughs
ready to burst into purple for that woman
who's been measuring my rose bed for a carport.

SONYA DORMAN

MAGIC CHILDREN

My children, you grow so
You make me feel like a joke,
A tiny car a lot of clowns
Climb out of.

How you multiply,
From none to three.
Your father and I must be
An old vaudeville act,
And life is quicker than the eye.

Rabbits, red and yellow scarves,
Fountains of paper flowers
Spring from you.
Doves disappear
In velvet curtains
Of your hair.

Oh, my magic children —
You saw me in two,
Are my bed of nails,
The burning coals I walk through,
Proof against wounds.

Loves, how shall I tell you
What I feel?
Like fans of cards,
Eternal and unreal,
We must all fold back
Into our own illusions.

BARBARA DRAKE

THE WIG

The short woman wearing the foot-tall wig
Who seems to have usurped a yellow hive
Suspects this is not quite the head's true home:
Her eyes will sometimes light with suppressed wings,
She fears mauling hands as if they were a bear's—
Only the passion to be someone different
Steadies her, and the knowledge that the brain
May well be incubating under hair.

So now her thoughts will have a yellow home;
They can come and go, well-pollinated—
There is synergy among her wishes.
One can almost sense the comb being filled.
We must stand near her, let the spirit hum,
Never regret the thousand flowers drained:
The dynamo beneath the cotton candy
Could have a revolution well in hand.

It may be sad at night to see the wig
Faceless on its form, no longer alive
With transformation, but this is the price
We must pay for such a revelation—
The woman asleep looks gray, passionless,
Tubercular with terror—Ecstasy
That set the cowl could not reveal the brain,
Lucid, thick with amber, crawling with bees.

CHARLES EDWARD EATON

A DROWNED VILLAGE

Below this gleam, between these mounds, there once,
The oldest people say, lived a village,
Which, for some sin, was cursed and drowned to death.
What the sin had been the local fables—
The gossip, the scandal—differed about.
The district archivist—the stirrer-up
Of discontent, enemy of progress—
Sighing (being short of breath) and shaking
His head (a nervous, family complaint),
Believed it was a refusal to hate
The beauty of the soil and the buildings—
To march with the times and accept the facts.
Others more spiritually minded—
The lunatic fringe, all of them on drugs—
Thought it was stubborn faith in the wrong god,
And the new god, in his anger, had called
The river to its ancient vocation—
The parish pump sunk by the Water Board.
Perhaps the false deity was Bacchus,
And modern soldiers had marched as to war,
Invaded the place and watered it down.
Perhaps it was Pan, and the same soldiers
Had thought it best the folk should play it cool.
Whatever the truth, the dwellers had paid
A high price for their secret wickedness.
The houses and the dancers, the postman,
The farm-workers, the schoolchildren, the church,
The store, the pub, the vicarage, had gone
Under the sea, all gone under the hill.
And it was a good thing too; for a town
Somewhere aloof thirsted with big new throats.

So, standing here, I think of a village
Which, after such time, had running water
And joined the main stream. Who is milking now
In the leaking shippons? Do the bats float

In the belfry still, and are there poor cats
Hallowing the adage? And what wild weeds
Sit swaying and guzzling in the saloon?
Is there the churching of mermaids? What form
Of prayer is used for those who die on land?
What new monster waits to be a legend?

And I watch the long light of silence creep
Across the lake, unshaken by the wind
Of change. Until, a stranger, I turn back,
Recalling the future. And as I trudge
Past the old men's beards hanging up to dry,
Through the wood where, in the early evening,
The roosters come to haunt another world,
Suddenly, beyond the water, I hear
A distant knocking sound, as though someone
Were making a new faith, meaning to move
To a new earth-home. And I wish him luck,
And all that is his for life, two by two.

JULIAN ENNIS

From

MAY DAY ROUNDS: RENFREW COUNTY

The stoop on the log-house is brown with sweet rain-rot
like the boards around an old pump   and the woman is afraid
she comes out of the daylight darkness of the little old house
like an ewe reflecting house-fire in her eyes   retreats
messages shouted back into the house   welfare is like sex
without love   it may be withdrawn at any time without reason
or notice   and then she moves to greet us   wiping her hands
on her faded apron   she is very afraid that we have come
to take something away   to make less in this single room
of cracked and worn linoleum and things without places
peeling unpainted   broken unmended   torn irreparable
work beyond woman's hands   and a nest of three hot irons
on the wood-stove for the week's wash   a man named Job
coughs behind the curtain and moves his feet restlessly in bed
the woman stands skitterish in the middle of the kitchen—
Jordan's voice reaches out to help—"How's your husband, Mrs. Clarke?"
"Oh, no better, I'm afraid. He's keepin' no better at all, at all" - - -
(Christ the Martyr, here is thy servant of the hot-stove
hands wring over this wretched fortune and hearken an old pain
going back into the childhood nails of our hands and feet)
"The children are all at school"   "Oh, yes, indeed, indeed - - - -"
"And how are they doing?"   "Oh, none too badly, I guess - - -"
she switches the frying pans of green bacon on the stove
the woman has only two biting teeth and an ironing-board back
age beyond all chronological reckoning including
this day's addition of fear   but something opens her pores
and flashes an earlier self now   it is when she finds
that we have not come to take anything away   "Oh, yes.
the Clarkes have been here a hundred years," she says
"that's my husband's family   three generations   did you see
the Century Sign on the gate?   the lawyer told us
one-hundred-and-twenty years   SHE HAS A MOMENT OF PRIDE
"I hear you grow apples here the size of pumpkins?"
she has ANOTHER moment standing by her cook-stove

with a battered array of potato-pots scoured and at-the-ready
"yes, yes, the Spy Apples like it here on the side
of the hill beside Lake Doré and our maple syrup was good
this year, too   let me give you some"   (she wants to reward us
for calling on her and not taking anything away)
we demur   she insists   and brings out a twelve-ounce whiskey bottle
full of the sweet spirits of the tall svelte vats
warm days and cold nights make love and sap come trickling down
we move towards her garden now   shelved along the small panes
a hundred-and-twenty years of moonlight and sunlight
falling on the floor and the faces of babies   school-boys
brides   mothers   dancers   cursers   lovers   wailers
givers   takers   weepers   singers   workers   coffin-bearers
fathers   sisters   brother   second-cousins   users   accusers
here this sainted shrine of scarlet geraniums and sweet pink clover
shoddies the room further and lights up her eyes   reaches out
and illuminates the manure piles   defies this stony heritage
the man coughs behind the curtain   he has nothing to say
all his prayers have gone unanswered   the three irons nest
hot on the cook-stove   the eldest son   aged twenty-one
is trapped here on this invisible farm   he is the sacrifice
on the mountain   alone in the barn he lets the cattle
have it with a pitch-fork

JOAN FINNIGAN

GHOST VILLAGE

Something takes me away, even from the spotlit
Indian clubs of our small happy government,
The gasp of hope and memory's applause,
In brown rooms, in yellow rooms, in red rooms by the sea,
To the colourless and soundless world we half-remember.

Presaged and annotated by our paltry sobs,
Older than all the lives we know or ever knew,
So sharply critical of the success of matter,
Keeping its own activities a deadly secret,
It is blind and alert as the black eyes of negatives.

Something said somewhere at some time is not enough
To appease its absorbing interest in what we did not mean
To old friends suddenly noticed as they glance up from books
With the sort of look which asks nothing because it is not worth it,
By the curled sea in rooms we shall half-forget.

Old friends in new rooms, new friends in old rooms:
It sees them come and go, because it is not worth it,
But a path down the valley cracked with grass
Brings us to the ghosts who must be faced.
Who questioned the blind world and would not let it lie.

Ghosts have hunters, but the hunters lose the track,
For the craned neck does not suspect a reply
And the star or the heron is never asked if it requires
To be looked at, by those who glance up from books
When the curtains are drawn back from the evening sky.

Friendless, rootless by choice, they made a home for this bay
Where pairs of stone windows were set to frown at the sea
With all the gloomy unconcern of self-absorbed exiles
Whose delineation of the jealousies and dribbled ghylls
Only betrayed their real longing and peculiar laughter.

Did neighbours wonder at the striding, the leaping of gates?
Did Squire Tribute, coming from beyond the ridge
Where the harnessed pismire superb in its plumes of dust
Pretended to be a horse on a careless errand,
Judge? Or was it changed, the outside world?

When Mistress Tidings courted Sinful the Silent
And whispers sent sidling three sides of the square
Returned across the gap, shocked and delighted,
Was it too much like what had always been known
To make much sense, the inside world?

For we have known that difference as well,
Hands drumming impatiently on green baize
As we listen to the next to last report,
The tank brimming, the wipers running freely,
Set for the coast and the foul pinks of love.

They took the mountain for its broken counterpart.
Steamers visited the creaking pier and the washed gravel
Lay heaped like wheat on the shore of their closed lives.
In front rooms hands were folded on knees. A ticking clock
Enlarged the stone silences, defining a central gravity.

They saw the cow turn her tail into a handle,
Replenishing three or four fields beside a cliff,
And resolved as they walked alone at evening in watchchains
To make their lives acceptable to others, their deaths
Only to themselves. And the fields steamed with joy.

Their children were the first to make shy advances,
Wove with fingers, were pinioned, wept, touched,
Cruelly accused the unhappy of being only unhappy,
Talked incessantly of the marriage of headland and valley
And thought of nothing much to say, but learned to read.

Until one day these became themselves the brooding exiles,
The best cap square set or the downed pick at noon,
The mountain unshaped with interjections of dynamite,

Tired of responsibility, dreaming, easily wounded,
Crying out to be, and being, successfully lured by cities.

Nothing is changed, and most of the dancing is still glum
In neighbouring villages where they watch and wait
For the silver band to assemble in the Sunday dusk.
Nothing is changed, when wishes are fulfilled
And again we stare into the boiling centre.

Nothing is changed, but everything will alter
And the blind world exults as we expect it should
Over the first and last, the inside and the outside,
The forms and secrets, friends and generations,
Pacts made by ghosts that some of us have tried to love.

So thinking, a tiny swivelling figure in the bay,
Hands in pockets, turning over stones with a holiday foot,
Posed between the unravelling tides and the abandoned houses,
Made an uncertain gesture, ceased watching the sea,
And plodded up the hill for company.

JOHN FULLER

NOAH, AFTER DIVINE RECONSIDERATION

It is upon us; the flood is upon us. Take to ship,
if there is a ship, because, most certainly,
the flood is upon us, or it seems to be;
or, at least, the western sky is darkening,
with no light coming from the East horizon.
Or, at least, if there is a light, it is too early
or we are too westerly to see it yet.
Take to ship, if there is a ship. I think
I see rainclouds, rather, I think it feels like rain,
and my grandmother thinks it feels like rain. She is seldom wrong,
or, at least, she is often right. Was there someone assigned
to regulate boarding, if we are to board?
It is awfully cold for rain; can one drown in snow?
Should we perhaps board farther south, does anyone know?—
or stay here, and take to snowshoes?—that is,
if the flood is upon us. The sky seems dark,
and birds are riccotting southward; the sky is full of birds,
perhaps, after all, it is they who are causing the darkness,
or perhaps I was right in saying the flood is upon us,
in which case, we should definitely take to ship.
Was anyone assigned
to find one, or build one? But this dampness could be the coming
of morning, if there is indeed a light
out of the east; it may be too early
or we may be too westerly to tell
if day is coming. Was anyone assigned
to tell the difference between day and drowning?
If so, perhaps we should set out to find him,
or set out to see if we should take to ship,
if the flood is upon us, as it almost appears to be.

SUZANNE GORDON

THE SEASON, ALREADY GONE

Here is sorrow we cannot expiate
or cure: the bitterness of the cores of green apples,
the smell of the rain on green apples
fallen too soon, after storms, fallen
on barren ground, on misers' ground, on stone.
My brother, you have been alone
since birth, when the seer and the midwives agreed
that the day was bad and too early.
that the day was early, and you would fall
on barren ground, the ground of misers, on stone.

Here, sorrow we cannot expiate, the rites
being lost, the sacrament of innocence
lost: in the orchard—remember—the dead tree
and the swing that carried you up
and took you to the north side of the wide creek
where Leda lay and Ophelia passed, still floating.
But you are not loved by a god nor a grieving wildman.
And you are neither swan enough nor saviour
enough to find new rites of expiation.
Your daughters will cause no fire, your death less sorrow.

The rain comes early and all the trees are losing
fruit too soon. The loam will be sweet
for some other planting. The old tree will go.
This is the season the creek will flood
the south bank, and the old tree will go.
Remember: the smell of apples after rain
and the feel of swinging over the cold creek,
the long drop to moss. Here is the sorrow
we cannot expiate or cure, the rites being lost:
this season gone too early in rain and this fruit rotting.

SUZANNE GORDON

THE MESSENGER

Is this man turning angel as he stares
At one red flower whose name he does not know,
   The velvet face, the black-tipped hairs?

His eyes dilated like a cat's at night,
His lips move somewhat but he does not speak
   Of what completes him through his sight.

His body makes to imitate the flower,
Kneeling, with splayed toes pushing at the soil,
   The source, crude, granular, and sour.

His stillness answers like a looking glass
The flower's, it is repose of unblown flame
   That nests within the glow of grass.

Later the news, to branch from sense and sense,
Bringing their versions of the flower in small
   Outward into intelligence.

But meanwhile, quiet and reaching as a flame,
He bends, gazing not at but into it,
   Tough stalk, and face without a name.

THOM GUNN

BLACK SQUIRRELS AND ALBERT EINSTEIN

Questioned as to the chiefest goal of science,
he sniffed, "To keep the scientist amused."
If he had said, "To grope toward God," they would have *known*
that he was crazy, even without
his accent and well-known pacifistic views.

. . . Communicated little those last years
even with his colleagues. Shunned underwear and haircuts—
and socks, because they only led to holes.
And who needs cuffs? He lopped them off to save on laundry.
No paper handy, he would lie abed
and scribble equations on the sheets.

    "The two-three times you might say we got chatty,
    all he talked about was squirrels—how ours
    in Mercer Street aren't like the ones in the old country.
    Kept repeating. Genius maybe, but he said
    almost the same things every time we met."

What *is* there you can say to strangers,
to the perennial strangers who live next door
and you see every day?
                    "Nice weather"?
                      "Hot enough
for you?"
            "Who do you pick to take the series?"
Or what's wrong with repeating? There are those
who love it. Homer, for all his "strong-greaved Achaians"
"Hector of the shiny helmet," "Apollo of
the silver bow," still holds his own in paperbacks.
                    Or take the case
of Mado, wondrous little whore girl, sweet
presence tinged with shades of Jules Pascin—
and loved her work. (Nothing is—unquote—
work unless you'd rather be doing something else.
Which never happened to her.) Still,

as the song asserts, "they don't make jam all night."
Man is a talking animal. But talk of what?
I tried bicycle races: she had never seen one.
Love: it was too much like talking shop.
Books: she had never read one.
Food: she was no gourmet. Clothes: she spent
her more meaningful moments not wearing any.
I lit on history—Louis Quatorze, at random.
He struck a spark. Louis Quatorze liberating
Brittany. (She came from Plougastel.)
Louis XIV and la petite O'Murphy.
Louis XIV and the retreat from Moscow.
Louis XIV and the rape of the Sabines.
Louis XIV and, oh! that Christmas night
crossing the rivière de la Loire to take
the drunken Hessians—des espèces de boches—
in the rear! Combining, as it did,
Christmas and boating, it was, next to
Louis XIV letting the old woman's cakes burn,
her favorite story. Encore! Encore!
and never change a word. Allons, encore.
   "Et le bon Roi lui dit, 'Bien merci, Mademoiselle
                                Pocahontas.
Tu m'as sauvé de la mort et du scalping.
Je te fais donc Contesse du Barry . . .' "
   "*Duchesse* du Barry! Tu vois que je ne dormais pas.
I only closed my eyes to listen better.
Encore. The one about the time he shot
the apple off the little Prince's head."

   "All he could talk about was squirrels. No kiddin'—
black squirrels with tufted ears!
Seems in the old country that's how they come."

                   RAMON GUTHRIE

FIRST OF ALL

First of all it is necessary
to find yourself a country
—which is not easy.
It takes much looking
after which you must be lucky.
There must be rocks and water
and a sky that is willing
to take itself for granted
without being overbearing.
There should be fresh fish
in the harbor, fresh bread
in the local stores.
The people should know
how to suffer without
being unhappy, and how to be happy
without feeling guilty. The men
should be named Dimitrios
Costa, John or Evangelos
and all the women should be
named Elena or Anthoula.
The newspapers should always
lie, which gives you something
to think about. There should be
great gods in the background
and on all the mountaintops.
There should be lesser gods
in the fields, and nymphs
about all the cool fountains.
The past should be always
somewhere in the distance
not taken too seriously
but there always giving perspective.
The present should consist of the seven
days of the week forever.
The music should be broken-hearted
without being self-indulgent.

It should be difficult to sing.
Even the birds in the trees should
work for a dangerous living.
When it rains there should be
no doubt about it. The people
should be hard to govern
and not know how to queue up.
They should come from the villages
and go out to sea, and go back
to the villages. There should be
no word in their language
for self-pity. They should be
farmers and sailors, with only
a few poets. The olive trees
and the orange trees and the cypress
will change your life, the rocks
and the lies and the gods
and the strict music. If you go there
you should be prepared to leave
at a moment's notice, knowing
after all you have been somewhere.

KENNETH O. HANSON

BALEARIC WINTER

All afternoon, the wind
has come from the sea to beat on the white walls
    of the island. The trunks of the Balearic pines
are bent from its force, and all day long
    I've thought of Chopin wintering on Majorca,
setting on paper the dainty marvels of his brain
    while the delicate webbed grip of his lungs
on the precious air grew slack and shallow,
    and he coughed, tried not to breathe, listened to rain.

Outside this room, the wind is fast and loud
against the windows and against the door
    that leads to our balcony. I sink in a chair
to work in the half light and whistle between my teeth
    a Chopin nocturne.

                    In the mornings here
the young *emigrés* from Europe and America
    sit outside a bar in the main square
or walk through the narrow white streets of the old city
    past doorways that lead to dark small rooms and windows
where caged birds sing. A boy and girl will sit
    in shelter against a wall, eating an orange.

Beside the road, daisies with yellow centres
    and single scarlet poppies are growing wild
among the almond trees, and by a white house
    the orange trees are thick and bright with fruit.

    In the afternoon, children walk on the beach
to gather shells, the miraculous common harvest
    of the shore, cowries, starfish, and all
the delicate architecture that is made
    and dies in the body of the sea, that children,
wise and willful, gather in the lust of beauty
    and carry away, carrying to closed rooms
the faint smell of the sea.

Beside this sea
shut up on Majorca, Chopin coughed in the rain
of the Balearic winter, an *emigré* writing down
melodic effete nocturnes and songs in praise
of Poland where he did not live. While Sand
comforted him and smoked and brooded and worked.

Late in the afternoon, the sun, bright as a poppy,
drops westward to the Atlantic, always westward,
like the gold that tempted west the burning eyes
of the conquistadors. Falling always, the sun
drops into the ocean, under the Atlantic
to the golden sensual underwater cities
that hang on the branches of the sea like oranges.

As the white walls darken and the island loses its gold,
the *emigrés* smoke drugs in tiny rooms.
I drink white wine and coffee, and I think
of those dainty effeminate fingers playing nocturnes
through all the wind and rain and fear of death
of that Majorcan winter.

DAVID HELWIG

CLAMMING AT ST. JAMES HARBOR

I

As I dragged the bullrake belted at my waist,
backed away, my weight against the chain,
my arms hauling at the crossbars,
and brought the basket up

filled with waterlogged driftwood, starfish,
stones, spidercrabs, snails, shells,
and sorted out the few clams
big enough to keep,

flounders scribbled ahead of their mud wakes,
schools of transparent minnows dotted
and dashed codes against my legs,
young eels kissed my sneakers

with words: this you shall always remember.
This water is the true blood, this
shore is the true body, this
sky the incarnate light.

II

Now, years later, perhaps walking, or reading,
or talking to someone I've long loved,
I leave my self to kneel
down at my own grave.

I kneel in a flat of the harbor at low tide, beside
a trench I've raked, facing the mill's oars
that now whirl down a lattice
of sun and shadow.

I hold relics in my arms: the jewelled claws of crabs,
strands of seaweed shining like saints' hair,
skates' eggs like black scarabs,
clamshells white as time's

waters could wash them. Each time now I kneel longer,
until the tide shall turn, the sun's red blade
drop, gulls fall from the night's tree
to my eyes like dark leaves.

WILLIAM HEYEN

BAPTISM

So pure the atmosphere!
Dead yellow leaves stream out like sparks in a gust
Flick, flick, in the bright sun.
Pale blue the sky all day,
Then the light sinks, leaving
Crystal greenness behind the thin webs of trees,
Long, long fading icy lucent eve:
Then a pure black with the stars in their right places.

The November day of sun had its own innocence,
Brevity, a barely warm touch on one's cheek.
Frisking through it my son with the long back,
Twelve-year-old dreamer, all eyes and grin
Who has chosen to be baptized today in the stone church
Lit and warm in the pure black dense night shadows.

In a blue and white robe he was the cynosure,
First bearing a candle with his hair damp from the font,
Then a cross, leading them all away. I was strangely
Not moved in any way in mesh with what was read
Or said, or even vowed by him in his light boy's voice,
Nor by Gibbon's anthem, nor even by the rectory cat,
Fawning about the pews, chased by his baby brother.
Nor even when we stood in line to lend our support and kneel.
On the soft clunch pillars are scrawled incomprehensible
Beginnings of words, graphic diagrams, scratches:
They made me gloomy: the day was so naked
With its pure sunlight, and is sombre now with the dark.
I wish I could commune with the ghost
Of my baptized boy: but the barriers
Are denser than stone between us: I love him,
But he's a colt, vague, clumsy, or larking:
There are moments that come to us, now and then, flashovers:
But between the child with the cross and the gloomy father,
I bewail a gulf that the simple autumn day mocks

With its light and darkness, its winds, its golden stripping.
Side by side, or hugging, makes it no better:
So separate, my son and I, and him carrying his high cross!

DAVID HOLBROOK

THE APPLE TREE

The seed spends a long time in the pit
Waiting at the center of the white flesh
For the fruit to ripen about it;
The root puts out endlessly its reach
Growing ever deeper into the dark,
Penetrating always further into the night;
The trunk holds all that went before,
By adding another inch to its girth
It preserves the memory of the past;
Branches go on dividing, avoid
Their destiny, coming to a conclusion
By increasing their complexities;
Leaves, like tongues or hands held out,
Are the shade under which the tree takes shelter;
Covered with dust, they endure hot and cold,
Rain and cracks of the parched earth
Through the long seasons of the year:
Only the time of the blossom is compressed
Into a brief span; the pink of the bud
Streaked with delicate veins of red,
Is consumed by the intensity of its life;
The sudden irresistible urge of the petals
That forces it so defenselessly to open,
And the white light of the incandescence
That then burns inside it.

THEODORE HOLMES

A FABLE

She dreamed of love coming to her as a fish
because for so long the hollow inside her
had resembled the liquid circle of a lake:
often she felt run through her little schools of fish,
and dreamed one day of them all joining into one.
Then she met him and to her surprise
as if it came down from heaven (for, in truth,
how else could it have got there)
there appeared on the water one day
a boat almost as large as the lake—
the gaily decked carnival ship of her marriage:
below the waterline the keel felt like a big fish.
And then the boat was no longer there
as if spirited away by the same hand that sent it,
leaving only the big fish: it kept coming and going
and sometimes when it went
she could feel its outlines in the water while she slept.
Then slowly her dreams changed to something more
permanent, to be erected on the bottom of the lake
more like the stately pleasure dome
that Kubla Khan decreed, than a big fish:
they sought as best they could to improvise it
by building around the shores of the lake—a porch,
a home, children, the golf club, Bridge, a boat—
thinking if they could ring it about with pleasures,
they could wall out its emptiness.
Then the boys grew up, the friends moved away,
their amusements began to fail, they sank deliberately
into ruts of their own, she grew old:
now at night when she goes down to the water
only the stars shine in the lake, water lights float
in the dark, the moon scatters its path of gold,
waves lap at the shore—that she once thought were
jewels, the decorations of something else,
she now knows are part of it
as the broken fragments of her soul.

And though the fish returns no more
but for the occasional smell of her origins in the sea,
the smell of fish oil sometimes in her nostrils at night,
they preserve the outward appearances of marriage,
punctilious attention to detail, measured
consideration, the civilized forms of estrangement,
keeping their meetings to a judicious minimum,
reserving them for entertainments, dinner, and going to bed:
as they grow further and further apart
the spaces between them have a peculiar nearness,
the way voices carry across water at night.

THEODORE HOLMES

CROW'S THEOLOGY

Crow realised God loved him—
Otherwise, he would have dropped dead.
So that was proved.
Crow reclined, marvelling, on his heart-beat.

And he realised that God spoke Crow—
Just existing was His revelation.

But what
Loved the stones and spoke stone?
They seemed to exist too.
And what spoke that strange silence
After his clamour of caws faded?

And what loved the shot-pellets
That dribbled from those strung-up mummifying crows?
What spoke the silence of lead?

Crow realised there were two Gods—

One of them much bigger than the other
Loving his enemies
And having all the weapons.

TED HUGHES

THE PLANET

From the center of the Sea of Tranquility—
a dry sea and a grainy—
see shining on the air
of that stretched night, a planet.

See it as serene and bright, very bright,
a far fair neighbor;
conceive what might be there
after the furious spaces.

Green fields, green fields,
oceans of grasses, breakers of daisies;
shadows on those fields,
vast and traveling,

the clouds' shadows.
And something smaller:
in the green grass, lovers, in each other's
arms, still, in the green.

The clouds will water the fields
the stream run shining
to the sea's motion; the sea shining
as the clouds travel and shine

so shine the daisies, as
the light in the seas
of the lovers' eyes. The innocent planet
far and simple, simple because far:

with lovers, and fields for flowers,
and a blue sky carrying clouds;
and water, water: the innocent planet,
shining and shining.

JOSEPHINE JACOBSEN

WAKING UP

I

On my right is a field of darkness.
The ants are busy in the tall grass.
I float on a lake of dark petals.

II

Waves of flesh wash over me.
I am looking into watery sky
At the bottom of an ancient well.

III

The field is flooded with darkness.
I sleep in curls of dark grass
Edged by a cloud of wild asters.

IV

A horse stands by a worm-eaten log.
It paws the dark with its right foreleg,
Cutting dark flowers in the air.

THOMAS JAMES

KING OF THE RIVER

If the water were clear enough,
if the water were still,
but the water is not clear,
the water is not still,
you would see yourself,
slipped out of your skin,
nosing upstream,
slapping, thrashing,
tumbling
over the rocks
till you paint them
with your belly's blood:
Finned Ego,
yard of muscle that coils,
uncoils.

If the knowledge were given you,
but it is not given,
for the membrane is clouded
with self-deceptions
and the iridescent image swims
through a mirror that flows,
you would surprise yourself
in that other flesh
heavy with milt,
bruised, battering towards the dam
that lips the orgiastic pool.

Come. Bathe in these waters.
Increase and die.

If the power were granted you
to break out of your cells,
but the imagination fails
and the doors of the senses close
on the child within,

you would dare to be changed,
as you are changing now,
into the shape you dread
beyond the merely human.
A dry fire eats you.
Fat drips from your bones.
The flutes of your gills discolor.
You have become a ship for parasites.
The great clock of your life
is slowing down,
and the small clocks run wild.
For this you were born.
You have cried to the wind
and heard the wind's reply:
"I did not choose the way,
the way chose me."
You have tasted the fire on your tongue
till it is swollen black
with a prophetic joy:
"Burn with me!
The only music is time,
the only dance is love."

If the heart were pure enough,
but it is not pure,
you would admit
that nothing compels you
anymore, nothing
at all abides,
but nostalgia and desire,
the two-way ladder
between heaven and hell.
On the threshold
of the last mystery,
at the brute absolute hour,
you have looked into the eyes
of your creature self,
which are glazed with madness,
and you say

he is not broken but endures,
limber and firm
in the state of his shining,
forever inheriting his salt kingdom,
from which he is banished
forever.

STANLEY KUNITZ

BEING AND BECOMING

I am becoming a ghost if it is possible
to become what I have always been.

I can tell. My arms had drifted off
some weeks ago, three weeks at least,
and my stomach gone for quite a time
but now, tonight, walking from your house
at two a.m., I felt my feet evaporate
and knew the truth. I am becoming

a ghost. A no-footed haunter. Spooks
will be my intimates, my grim consolers,
and I will find my truest self. Person
to person. But that will have to wait.

Right now I am in process. Once the legs
have gone, the head, the stupid torso,
once the heart has whisked along the street
as soot or ashes or a nuisance in the eye,
I shall desist. I shall be the ghost I am.

But you, alchemist, I shall forget you never.

JOHN L'HEUREUX

EPPUR SI MUOVE

I was thinking of Galileo the other night.
As usual. What a nerve the old bastard had
To bow his head before a phalanx of caped fools
And say I'm sorry gentlemen my mistake
Like the chairman of the board
With all the shareholders showing their fangs
After a fall in the index.
No drama or martyred bones for history's bobbysoxers
And their loud laments. He needed time
To bring his little telescope to bear
Upon the planets and the puffed cant
Of all the demons in their red peaks
Who had the world in order neat as a sewing box.

I can see him fiddling at the window
And cursing from an overdose of Latin blood
The damned irregularities of globes in their hot spots
A wandering foam of ignorance and ether
And jabbing pins on cardboard every time
That Jupiter could offer up a ball
Of shadow as his brood of moons
Skipped around his fat night grin
Like a ping-pong quadrille to the music of the stars.
And when he had the evidence he shoved it up
Like the senior chef in a four star pub
Offering with his bland hands a confident dish
Of several hours' invention
Spiced with a secret gravy.

Can you blame the cold cardinals
Stuck on their smooth arses in a ton of silk
Primed with the word of a leaky Jew
And every ghost tale of a sulphurous testament
Bristling under apprehensive eyes
When this heretic scribbler
Spiked their red singlets with his juicy quills

Like a randy porcupine in the bushes
An intellectual poker jiving with the peaceful ash
Of a cosy fire place and a cool routine.

And they paid for it of course. They always do.
When someone like this cunning crank comes on
And fusses with the backstage of the universe
The top dogs lose their nerve if he keeps it up.
And from the sunken palace of his own detention
In the prison of a thousand days
He knew he'd beaten them and pushed
The frightened conmen into one false move.

Every word he smuggled out was one more puncture
In the canister of truth they'd sealed from sight.
Because the anxious clerics hadn't got the guts
To burn the old weasel no matter what
Before he caught them at their stacked game.
He just wasn't a glamorous Joan
Who'd step up on the pyre and thank his happy God
For a chance to feel the flames
At his varicose ankles taking the tan away.
No sir. Tell the old turds a few fibs
And get on with the job at state expense.

PETER LOFTUS

THE CHINESE GREENGROCERS

They live their days in a fragrance
of white and black grapes
and tomatoes and the fresh
water smell of lettuce.

They know with their hands
and noses the value
of all things grown.
They will make you a bargain price
on overripe canteloupe.

They wash with clear water
their bunches of carrots
and radishes. They crank out
a canvas awning to shelter them.

Their babies suckle on unsold bananas.
By the age of six
they can all make change
and tell which fruits are ripe.

The grandmothers know only numbers
in English, and the names
of fruits and vegetables.

They open before the supermarkets open,
they are open all day,
they eat with an eye on the door.

They keep sharp eyes
for shoplifting children.
They know every customer's
brand of cigarettes.

After the neighbourhood movies are out
and the drugstores have all closed

they bring in their blueberries
and cabbages and potted flowers.

In the rooms behind the store
they speak in their own language.
Their speech flies around the rooms
like swooping, pecking birds.

Far into the night I believe
they weigh balsa baskets
of plums, count ears of corn
and green peppers.

No matter how they may wash
their fingers, their very pores
are perfumed with green,
and they sleep with parsley and peaches
oranges and onions
and grapes and running water.

PAT LOWTHER

PENELOPES

1

When we see the dancer
move her slim form
in speech purer than speech,

we do not see the muscles strain
and reach;

we do not think of years unlearning
earth's hard facts,
or of the sweat it takes
to break the pattern the mind makes
of stone and apple-fall;
or how the will is set and firm
in snipping the tough warp of gravitation,

leaving space to conceive her body's acts
of delicate free levitation.

2

Admiring a XIVth century arras,
woven perhaps by some less faithful dame,
we see a gentle fable of the time:
virgin and unicorn on silken grass.

The shapely doll-house landscape stands bemused;
the beast, a sublimate of darker gods,
moves ceremoniously. Beyond the woods
the hunter's hounds stand marble-still, confused.

Tracing the symmetry of peacock trees
eyed with such fruit as gardens never grew,
we can be charmed and, half-amused, agree
about that other time's naiveties

Yet, in the ancient stitched design not see
the twin duplicity depicted here,
as maid and unicorn approach the hour
which all their patterned lives would make them flee:

How stealthily the girl must loose her fears
of horn, and of its fleshy referent,
and all imagining of brute affront,
that innocence may be as it appears.

And how the timid unicorn, all taut
with nerves that know the smallest shift of leaf,
must now renounce all learning of his life,
and wilfully walk forward to be caught.

3

    When I was Penelope
  I lived
  for the one gold day
  in a winter's rain

unravelled every night
what I had learned of pain
I searched for the faces of friends and lovers
    on buses
         in the street crowd
secretly
I was proud
  I could make one
  fat drop of sun
    burst its warm juices on my head.

So prized and lovely that,
  it could sustain
  my work of slyly tearing, thread by thread
  what I had learned

of enemies
  and the heart's maze

and the demon-perilled journey between
first   and second thought

4

So the old boy came home,
burst brawling into the anteroom,
interrupting forever covert yawns
scurrilous anecdotes
    sweet songs—

the place at once a melee of kicked bums,
hacked limbs,
slimy with blood of those who hadn't been quick
or didn't bounce far enough on the first kick—

Blood to the elbows, he howled:
"Woman, where in hell's my towel?"

He believed her finally, and her slaves;
examined the tapestry the wove and unwove;
accepted her as loyal;

but there was distance in his eyes,
veiled inattention she had come to recognize
in suitors, begging her for loving looks
while mentally counting vines and flocks.

He dozed over wine,
made love indifferently;

his eyes kept turning, sucking, to the sea;
he would start, "Did I tell you about the time—"

then shrug, and go out to gossip with his men.

In a matter of weeks
he was off again

and Penelope, left with her flawed work
had it to face:

She could have spun her hanging of her hair
or made her bed a market thoroughfare—
he didn't care.

And it came to a choice:
whether to let her age-long labour fall,
grow old and bitter, turn her face to the wall,
or somehow to gather will,
begin picking the pattern of her life,
and weave again
            designs
                        of innocence and disbelief . . .

PAT LOWTHER

A LAST DIALOGUE: MOSES

Father, I have gone through
Those seven places you call Faith
And I have managed.
Now age, particulars,
The cold exception of the wind
Hold me to this rock.
This Moab.
I did not crave this journey,
Others had more eloquence,
Longer faith. And when
You stretched a land before us,
A separate place of rumored
Milk and honey—I was afraid.

With plagues as thick as law,
We ran from Egypt, armies fast
Upon our heels, till there,
Collected by flat water,
We waited for the thick Red
Sea to group, to pass into
The wind, heard Pharoah curse
And drown, his soldiers drown again.

Your word, my stone:
From that mountain I descended.

Saw your lion crouched
In ghettos
Whimper like disaster for a name,
A molten calf that damned us
Faithfully.

I split a kingdom
For our thirst—
No rock was worth that price!
Now you call me here

To bargain faith, to show me
Canaan, its green plains far
Below; the olives, fat and ripe
That shimmer from the trees.
Is heaven more than that?

I lean into mortality.

ADRIANNE MARCUS

From

FOUR FOR THEODORE ROETHKE

IV

THE BURDEN

The burden, flowering, at heavy cost:
He knew the cost, knew how the burgeoning
Bough shudders in the wind, an anxious ghost—
And the heavy price paid when the opening
Buds become the blossoms on a tree;
Those blossoms ripen and they break their bough.

No longer pacing out his middle age,
He tumbled quickly to an ecstasy,
He loosened into love, that purest rage,
Impossible to risk, or justify:
Circumference was never more than here
And now, no end was on it, anywhere—

There was no edge, there was no edge at all!
He knew the virtue of some secret name,
It was impossible for him to fall:
Bobbing like a blossom on a stem
He was indifferent to all but joy,
And with his words he gave himself away;

Inside the cherry is the lightest stone,
But nonetheless the cherry's branches cry
Out at its weight: they cannot bear for long
The burden of their joy. No more could he.
That heavy body bore a glistening word.
Now fold his hands away, misunderstood.

CHARLES MARTIN

THE MONKEY'S PAW

When the war is over the bones of the lonely dead
will knit and rise from ricefield and foxfield
like sea-things seeking the sea, and will head
toward their homes in Hanoi or Seattle
clogging the seaways, the airways, the highways
climbing the cliffs and trampling the clover
heading toward Helen, Hsueh-ying, or Mary
when the war is over

When the war is over Helen, Hsueh-ying, or Mary
and lonely women all over the world
will answer the knock on the door like that insane story
and find on their doorstep something they used to hold
in their arms, in their hearts, in their beds
and that something will reach out and crumble
and the eyes cave back in the head
when the war is over

When the war is over curses will mount in the air
like corbies, to flock over capitol cities
and flutter and hover and waver and gather
till white buildings turn black beneath their cloud
and then they will drop like bombs, talons
zeroed in on the dead hearts still walking around
on the ground with memos in their briefcases
when the war, when the war is over

PETER MEINKE

THE JUDGMENT OF PARIS

Long afterward
the intelligent could deduce what had been offered
and not recognized
and they suggest that bitterness should be confined
to the fact that the gods chose for their arbiter
a mind and character so ordinary
albeit a prince

and brought up as a shepherd
a calling he must have liked
for he had returned to it

when they stood before him
the three
naked feminine deathless
and he realized that he was clothed
in nothing but mortality
the strap of his quiver of arrows crossing
between his nipples
making it seem stranger

and he knew he must choose
and on that day

the one with the gray eyes spoke first
and whatever she said he kept
thinking he remembered
but remembered it woven with confusion and fear
the two faces that he called father
the first sight of the palace
where the brothers were strangers
and the dogs watched him and refused to know him
she made everything clear she was dazzling she
offered it to him
to have for his own but what he saw
was the scorn above her eyes

and her words of which he understood few
all said to him *Take wisdom*
take power
you will forget anyway

the one with the dark eyes spoke
and everything she said
he imagined he had once wished for
but in confusion and cowardice
the crown
of his father the crowns the crowns bowing to him
his name everywhere like grass
only he and the sea
triumphant
she made everything sound possible she was
dazzling she offered it to him
to hold high but what he saw
was the cruelty around her mouth
and her words of which he understood more
all said to him *Take pride*
take glory
you will suffer anyway

the third one the color of whose eyes
later he could not remember
spoke last and slowly and
of desire and it was his
though up until then he had been
happy with his river nymph
here was his mind
filled utterly with one girl gathering
yellow flowers
and no one like her
the words
made everything seem present
almost present
present
they said to him *Take*
her
you will lose her anyway

it was only when he reached out to the voice
as though he could take the speaker
herself
that his hand filled with
something to give
but to give to only one of the three
an apple as it is told
discord itself in a single fruit its skin
already carved
To the fairest

then a mason working above the gates of Troy
in the sunlight thought he felt the stone
shiver

in the quiver on Paris's back the head
of the arrow for Achilles' heel
smiled in its sleep

and Helen stepped from the palace to gather
as she would do every day in that season
from the grove the yellow ray flowers tall
as herself

whose roots are said to dispel pain

W. S. MERWIN

THUNDER

Across the garden, empty deck chairs
Arranged in friendly groups,
Knees touching, exchanging whispers.
The wind strengthens in their sails,
Flapping them nowhere, irritably,

And the guests have all gone indoors
In case of thunder, huddling close
Like mirrors admiring each other.
Outside, rain gust and light
Flash across the grass.

We must cover up all shining objects.
The storm will break them. See
In the lightning the glasshouse
Whitens suddenly, unable to move,
Its glass world exposed and terrified.

In the city, people with glass skulls
Are struggling home. Walls, clothes
Of glass. Glass bodies, paling
Of colour as the sky darkens.
In doorways, those that are sheltering

Are doing glass things, delicate hands
Polishing their reflected selves,
Then, growing silent and anxious.
I look at my hands, they have
Already grown shiny, shaped with age.

And as the raged sky strikes out
I see nothing to shelter me,
And nothing to shelter, reflecting all.
And my own brittle body, careful on the earth
Which is still the earth, green and still, appeased.

PAUL MILLS

EARLY FROST

We were warned about frost, yet all day the summer
Has wavered its heat above the empty stubble. Late
Bees hung their blunt weight,
Plump drops between those simplest wings, their leisure
An ignorance of frost.
My mind is full of the images of summer
And a liquid curlew calls from alps of air;

But the frost has come. Already under trees
Pockets of summer are dying, wide paths
Of the cold glow clean through the stricken thickets
And again I feel on my cheek the cut of winters
Dead. Once I awoke in a dark beyond moths
To a world still with freezing,
Hearing my father go to the yard for his ponies,

His hands full of frostnails to point their sliding
To a safe haul. I went to school,
Socks pulled over shoes for the streets' clear glass,
The early shops cautious, the tall
Classroom windows engraved by winter's chisel,
Fern, feather, and flower that would not let the pale
Day through. We wrote in a cold fever for the morning

Play. Then boys in the exulting yard, ringing
Boots hard on winter, slapped with their polishing
Caps the arrows of their gliding, in steaming lines
Ran till they launched one by one
On the skills of ice their frail balance,
Sliding through time with not a fall in mind,
Their voices crying freely through such shouting

As the cold divided. I slid in the depth
Of the season till the swung bell sang us in.
Now insidious frost, its parched grains rubbing
At crannies, moved on our skin.
Our fingers died, not the warmth

Of all my eight wide summers could keep me smiling.
The circle of the popping stove fell still

And we were early sped through the hurrying dark.
I ran through the bitterness on legs
That might have been brittle, my breath
Solid, grasping at stabs of bleak
Pain to gasp on. Winter branched in me, ice cracked
In my bleeding. When I fell through the teeth
Of the cold at my haven door I could not see

For locked tears, I could not feel the spent
Plenty of flames banked at the range,
Nor my father's hands as they roughed the blue
Of my knees. But I knew what he meant
With the love of his rueful laugh, and my true
World unfroze in a flood of happy crying,
As hot on my cheek as the sting of this present

Frost. I have stood too long in the orderly
Cold of the garden, I would not have again the death
Of that day come unasked as the comfortless dusk
Past the stakes of my fences. Yet these are my
Ghosts, they do not need to ask
For housing when the early frost comes down.
I take them in, all, to the settled warmth.

LESLIE NORRIS

LOVING

A balloon of gauze around us,
sheerest gauze: it is a balloon of skin
around us, fine light-riddled skin,
invisible.

If we reach out to pinch its walls it floats from us—
it eludes us wetly, this sac.

It is warmed by a network of veins
fine as hairs and invisible.
The veins pulsate and expand to the width
of eye-lashes.
In them blood floats weightless as colour.
The warm walls sink upon us when we love
each other, and are blinded by the heavier skin
that closes over our eyes.

We are in here together.
Outside, people are walking in a landscape—
it is a city landscape, it is theirs.
Their shouts and laughter come to us in broken sounds.
Their strides take them everywhere in daylight.
If they turn suddenly toward us we draw back—
the skin shudders wetly, finely—
will we be torn into two people?

The balloon will grow up around us again
as if breathed out of us, moist and sticky and light
as skin, more perfect than our own skin,
invisible.

JOYCE CAROL OATES

SALMON

for Ceri Richards

The river sucks them home.
The lost past claims them.
    Beyond the headland
It gropes into the channel
Of the nameless sea.
    Offshore they submit
To the cast, to the taste of it.
It releases them from salt,
Their thousand miles in odyssey
For spawning. It rehearsed their return
    From the beginning; now
    It clenches them like a fist.

    The echo of once being here
    Possesses and inclines them.
        Caught in the embrace
    Of nothing that is not now,
    Riding in with the tide-race,
        Not by their care,
    Not by any will they know,
    They turn fast to the caress
    Of their only course. Sea-hazards done,
    They ache towards the one world
        From which their secret
        Sprang, perpetuate

More than themselves, the ritual
Claim of the river, pointed
    Towards rut, casting
Their passion out. Weeping philosopher,
They re-affirm the world,
    The stars by which they ran,
Now this precise place holds them
Again. They reach the churning wall
Of the brute waterfall that shed

Them young from its cauldron pool.
  A hundred times
  They lunge and strike

  Against the hurdles of the rock;
  Though hammering water
      Beats them back
  Still their desire will not break.
  They coil and whip and kick,
      Tensile for their truth's
  Sake; give to the miracle
  Of their treadmill leaping
  The illusion of the natural.
  The present in torrential flow
      Nurtures its own
      Long undertow:

They work it, strike and streak again,
Filaments in suspense.
  The lost past shoots them
Into flight out of their element,
In bright transilient sickle-blades
    Of light; until upon
The instant's height of their inheritance
They chance in descant over the loud
Diapasons of flood, jack out of reach
And snatch of clawing water,
    Stretch and soar
    Into easy rapids

Beyond, into half-haven, jounce over
Shelves upstream; and know no question
    But, pressed by their cold blood,
Glance through the known maze.
They unravel the thread to source
    To die at their ancestry's
Last knot, knowing no question.
They meet under hazel trees
Are chosen and so mate. In shallows as

The stream slides clear, yet shirred
        With broken surface where
        Stones trap the creamy stars

Of air, she scoops at gravel with fine
Thrust of her exact, blind tail;
        At last her lust
Gapes in a gush on her stone nest
And his great squanderous peak
        Shudders his final hunger
On her milk; seed laid on seed
In spunk of liquid silk.
So in exhausted saraband their slack
Convulsions wind and wend galactic
        Seed in seed, a found
        World without end.

        The circle's set, proportion
        Stands complete and,
                Ready for death,
        Haggard they hang in aftermath
        Abundance, ripe for the world's
                Rich night, the spear.
        Why does this fasting fish
        So haunt me? Gautama, was it this
        You saw from river-bank
        At Uruvela? Was this
                Your glimpse
                Of holy law?

                JOHN ORMOND

SQUATTERS' RIGHTS

First we raked out the shatter of glass,
And fall of the silt of time from the floors.
Light let itself in, followed by the terrified
Air. The smell of roses by the door
Moved in, soft-shoe, like a pantomime Old Maid
Stiffened by sounds before they clapped and rattled.
Even the house felt, we half-sensed, afraid
Squatters might live here, lurking till after dark
To lay waste to our movings-in, to crash our
Pots and pans around our ears in the disturbed air.

And there *were* populations all around us.
Bats met. We could hear the convocation,
And the rise of their voices, and the breaking up,
The trailing away of their skirting wings between
Partitions. In the northeast corner they camp-met
And discussed us and revival-prayed nightly
For a whole summer, grey-robed and full of grace,
Questioning whether the Lord allowed us space.

In the southwest corner there was multiple scamper of feet,
Like a running of many excited little girls.
The back and forth was incredible, it was like
The borrowing of hair ribbons and the trying on
Of ladies' scarves and fans, the weaving of serial
Romances, and the brewing up of hexes till nearly dawn,
Their scurry knocked silly at a thought of life beyond them.
Thus we were accepted by the flying squirrels.

Now we all live together after a fashion,
An interlocking of mysteries, a reverence of musics:
We hear them, they hear us, — to us there is a music as
Of Chinese reeds and broken sleigh bells; they
May hear a thunder where we walk on aging boards,
And voices like the winds at holes in trees.

JEAN PEDRICK

SONG SPARROW

It is born in them   the untuned instrument
encased in bone a memory of sound
neither tone nor strict melodic line
the idea rather   the unformed expression
tormenting young birds cradled in soundproof rooms
dreaming of singing as they dream to fly

those deafened early are fortunate
language abandons them
the voice of ancestors strangles in the vault
under triple membranes
threads web and branch among deep ganglia
ghosts unheard are powerless to shake
treasuries of sunlight from imagined leaves
silent as trees under frozen water
the mind is spared rehearsal rituals
the endless prelude struggling for
unanimous response to life
climax and coda of the sparrow song
which once accomplished permits no evasion
from repetition and embellishment

birds deafened later retain purpose and pattern
calling wings on the wind over springgreen valleys
sunwarm wings over waterfall and stone
swinging the sky above the body
veils ribboning upwards blue blurred with rainbows

filling the prison the voice avalanches down icy walls
under the rubble of that terrible music
the brown bird calls and calls.

GRACE PERRY

IN THE SEQUOIAS' SHADE

You can never see their tops;
only how far the sky pours
down before the light greens off,
goes dark and then still darker,
branching into centuries.

Ants trickle down the frayed rust
of hand-deep furrows. You walk,
circling the great buttresses
made while men thought and unthought
themselves, until you trespass

on the lost floor of the world:
the way the old ones stand there,
holding their quiet, breathing,
becomes more than a gesture,
a final thing. You can sense,

almost, their treeness, almost
approach the poise that steadies
them, denying their regress
back to a seedling's clutch
unclutching, spent, in the slime

of accident. They are not
that, but simply what prevailed:
what fingered our lost bone hulks,
shreddings of worms, moles, shells,
mineral seepage of rocks,

the bitter mulch of their own
unleavings—all the debris,
death-rot of earth, has sweetened
their roots. And they stand lofty.
As if they had gripped, beyond

both themselves and us, something,
some last reserve of earth that,
shored and walled, rose to proclaim
itself—living in what they are,
refusing, needing nothing.

MARGARET PETERSON

BOY AND GIRL

Look across the road there, by the bus stop,
and you'll see them. They stand barricaded from their friends
waiting for the school bus. Half an hour
I've noticed them. I doubt if a word's been spoken.

But there is a terse caution in the bend of her neck,
in the way she looks at him. Something
curves out from her and whips back—
fragile as a thought, something half loving yet pugnacious.

And he is staring suspiciously, through his eyelashes.
Sinewy under the frail cloth, his body's
poised for the impossible act. The sunlight spills
hotly across the hard shoulders, the shy buttocks.

So that the woman walking her dog is forced
to veer to her right and not come too close,
and the man in the natty blue shirt is uncomfortable,
looks fixedly away from them, quickens his footsteps.

And the young married couple with the groceries—
even they are held by this weight of strangeness
and glance terror-struck at each other, in the middle
of what is, suddenly, no longer their own conversation.

Yet the boy and the girl have not moved. The distance
between them is such their fingertips could meet
if they could power their fingers, while abruptly beside them
jabbers the school bus, its brakes whistling with anger.

CRAIG POWELL

TREE AND RIVER BANK

Dead jacaranda flowers are more beautiful
the more they wrinkle into the soil. Alive
they're a staccato hissing purple, clattering their coloured beaks,
and even fallen they are vivid. I think they are
like the souls of old men, profoundly folding
to a mauve powder in the grass.

Joseph Edwin Makin, you were my grandfather:
the child I named for you is also dead.
Between your eighty-one years and his three weeks
I tread mid-life across a concrete bridge
spattered with jacaranda, gouging from the past
the peace caught in your cracked arthritic knuckles,
that darker peace fluent with your outbreathing:
who earned this peace by being old, when the jolt
of your heart-beat, stiff and cantankerous as my own,
calmed, and there was nothing you'd not learned to love.

But the footpath's hard here under my shoes, and the live
jacaranda blossoms spit and haggle beside a bridge
that hugs two identical banks. Whether to expect
the peace of old men or the peace of children
is a lure before which the soul is puzzled, halts,
grasping at neither one. Neither is offered.
Grandfather, there are like hoops around the jumping heart
bones and living nerve that must be torn
layer by angry layer
before that half-wished intolerable splendour.

Yet I step like you from the bridge onto the yielding earth
and the jacaranda's blue mist. Your death and my child's
I carry deep, as early and late darkness,
as ever-recurring pain. Beneath the sculpted bridge
the river glows among poplars and I can see fish
dive to the cold thoughts of water like white stones.

CRAIG POWELL

THE BRIDEWELL DISPUTE

They got on like a house on fire. All the rooms furnished alike.
Suites of fire, fire armchairs
Like golden fluttering birds in cages
Seated round the incandescent grate,
Chair-fires drawn up around the blazing tables.
Light flaring curtains agreeing with summer outside
Shone over windowpanes that agreeing with the sunny air
Kindled and blew out burning hot.
Dresses all in the same fashion were pouring light
From all the fiery wardrobes, in the kitchen
The knives and forks got on together
Agreeing with the spoons, brimmed dresser drawers,
Fell through together, splashed together
By the gas-stove shining like a maned chrysanthemum
And sheer-white steam shooting from the taps that ran
In glittering lead like water. Flowering fire
Coursed its crepitating colours through the greenhouse,
Carpets, linen-cupboards, books and portraits
Died into red and tarry black together,
Puffed into flocks like mating butterflies
Of jet black that flew up high, together.
Ceilings met floors and agreed their dark foundations,
And a mud arose, a mud of air mixed with their possessions,
Staining the summer air with all their best
In one swash and flex of the pluming apparition
Of burning house, all agreeing
To darken summer as far as possible with their best,
And like a house on fire, faded on the windroads.

PETER REDGROVE

VISIONS

Each day poised over banalities, his dismayed
Brain swayed and tugged and in its high empty spaces
Made visions of calm returns to lost places;

Sometimes he turned up smiling on an old bike,
Sometimes took a fast train and a short walk,
But most often he slipped languidly from a black car;

A cry of recognition and one rose to unclick the door
And held out a hand that was not too firm, the eyes
Seeking pardon, a plea behind the conventional words;

He replied—it didn't matter what he replied;
There was some reason or other for his being there,
Implied the wished forgiveness wryly, his generosity clear;

Then looked about him with relish at the unchanged past,
Ran upstairs, touched everything, enjoyed himself;
These fantasies gave him a faint smile over invoices;

In bed, though, his dream balloon, unhitched, was less reliable,
The chauffeur was truculent, the bicycle fell to pieces,
And the trains, if he caught them, landed him miles from anywhere;

He often woke sweating from these night parodies,
Then sank into worse nightmares, of being cast out
By appalling words and a limp hand into a desert

Which was his without question, his inheritance, each harsh
Stone scrawled with a price, and at the horizon
Receding cities of meaning that mocked his stumbling.

COLIN ROBINSON

HOME AGAIN

Propelled through time and space,
We make re-entry here;
Breathe a known atmosphere.

Nothing is out of place,
And yet we find it all
Alien, inscrutable.

It seems we must accept
The shape things draw on air
Merely by being there:

The faded walls, adept
At letting criss-cross books
Paper over the cracks,

The stolid easy chair
That sags like a stone sill
Or worn memorial.

Since with this world we share
An old complicity—
We brought it to be—

Why is the look so strange
On mine, or my child's face,
Caught in a looking-glass?

What base yet out of range
Can send instructions now
How to make contact; how?

PETER SCUPHAM

HE WHO REMAINS

you have so much to give they said
so I gave it now it is gone

I stand with my back to a cliff
where stones lean over
looking down at me they are smooth
they have dragged themselves
a long way to get here

years ago I wrote love letters
to distant water and wore
the desire to travel like a hair shirt

but that is over and regret
was never a friend of mine so I
let him go in search of the others

who departed wearing accidental lives
mocking me calling me *he who remains*

and I remain in the desert
caught in the ropes of myself like
rosaries staying here with penitent
stars whose confessions frighten me

there is no explanation for lights
which move about inside the mountains
and coyotes are all that is left
of a race we once conquered

at night I hear them worshipping
gods with unspeakable names

I have learned to make use of pain
he never fails to take me

into his confidence telling me
more than I wanted to know

and when morning arrives bringing
whatever it can to help I ready myself
for the impetuous revival of sand

if I were to leave this desert
who would cherish transparent
light who would nurse broken stones
who would mother the cold

RICHARD SHELTON

VALEDICTION

I who witnessed the nail's desire
for a blind hammer
and kept account books of rain

have got through the day without hope
what an accomplishment
now I can drop my eyes like stones
in the black water of night

I am taking myself apart
like a puzzle

this must be an ear this must be
a piece of my coat
or is it sky which there is so much of
and all the same color

I am resigning from my shoes
they are worn out
and will fit anybody

whoever wears them
his job will be to harvest
the delicate shells of walnuts

he must remember the signals
how to speak
to ducks about their carelessness
how to remind trees they have
a certain responsibility

he must prevent the sleepy road
from stumbling into the river
and watch for tiny fish
who swim past
carrying great burdens of light

RICHARD SHELTON

SOMEWHERE, BETWEEN THE FIRST BREATH
AND THE LAST

Somewhere, between the first breath and the last,
You will pause in crowded light or in darkness
Along a street of no local colour (as if a hand
Withheld you from encroaching air):
Estranged, with reality hanging as a threadbare memory,
You stop: become the unknown voice,

The hands, the heart and eyes of someone
You have never been, or will never be again
Beyond this transient moment of incomprehension
And bewildered acknowledgment.
You ask: but how long this wait, for the answer
To a question that is but a turning of thought:

Such a movement and displacement of sense
That logic can only mumble out a phrase
About footsteps walking over your grave, and sunlight
Or darkness become oblique shapes of emptiness:
Those borderless contours of space which are neither
Skyway nor ground, angular or level.

Yet it will pass, like an angel of death
That has erred upon that frightful journey—
                              the brief,
The sudden and terrific impact of identity passes,
And no more the rush of blood, cold and heavy as quicksilver:
Only yourself, from outside and deep within, seen
In a frame that holds what is neither mirror nor portrait.

                    PETER SKRZYNECKI

MATTER OF IDENTITY

Who he was, remained an open question
He asked himself, looking at all those others—
The strangers, roaring down the street—

Explorer, politician, bemedalled
General, teacher—any of these
He might have been. But he was none.

Impossible, though, to avoid the conclusion
That he had certain attributes: for instance,
Parents, birthday, sex. Calendars

Each year the same day added up his age.
Also he was a husband and had children
And fitted in an office, measure of his desk.

Yet he never felt quite certain
Even of certainties: discerned a gap
(Like that between two letters) between statistics

(These he was always writing out on forms)
And his real self. Sometimes he wondered
Whether he had ever been born, or had died . . .

(A blank space dreaming of its asterisks)
    *   *   *

Sometimes he had the sensation
Of being in a library and reading a history

And coming to a chapter left unwritten
That blazed with nothing . . . nothing except him.
—Nothing but his great name and his great deeds.

STEPHEN SPENDER

CLOVES

1

Whatever my enemies find, I have to face—
taste that false man who provides
my world, myself. That clove turns real:
they are right.

2

I try to eat the subtle mushroom
arched through all that the world gives me;
then fear surfaces. I taste clove,
the great reality under the earth.

3

Here in the now part of history, bundled
together in these rooms, blinded and dumb
so that we can last without shrilling
upward and out—suddenly aware, I bite clove.

4

When out of the bland hours we let come
to us a start that makes us religious,
it is church, wherever it is: we bite clove
even while we speak our mild sentences.

5

You and I come different ways to every
hill, and cross at paths that never
will be finally the same. There is
a clove we step on, passing.

6

When you travel, scenes follow you
all night, pressing lightly on your
lips, and your country is only the one
lasting in the accent of your denials.

WILLIAM STAFFORD

A BIRTHDAY

On the morning of my birthday I awoke from a dream
Where I came down from walking in a park on a hill.
The hill had two sides: on one the bright chaparral
Stood separate and shining on the brown hay of summer
On the other, pineshade—and ferns on the floor of a forest.
They vanish away as smoke in the air.

The ground was soft underfoot
It was evenly planted; all things were in order.
I was barefoot, and it was holiday
And I came down and found the streets full of people
And I walked in full and swinging skirts among them.
He is great that sets at nought all worldly honor.

Beloved, we go west to the wide sea
All of us, coming down from the hill.
All of us, all, borne on the shell of earth—
Though far from the sea you ride.
And I may behold all things as they be, of short abiding.

At my center is a pool, calm
Dark. I have not found its edges.
And as I turn westward
Though I have not found wisdom
The great pool of peace is the center, what I am and that only.
May nothing take from thee inward liberty of soul.

In this first morning of my year I awoke
And all things were hung with light.

ANN STANFORD

THE FATHERS

I am beset by spirits, layer on layer
They hover over our sleep in the quilted air.
The owl calls and the spirits hang and listen.
Over our breaths, over our hearts they press.
They are wings and eyes, and they come surely to bless
There is hardly room for the crowd of them under the ceiling.

Remember me, remember me, they whisper.

The dark rustles, their faces all are dim.
They know me well, I represent them here.
I keep their lands, their gold and fruiting orchards,
I keep their books, their rings, their testaments.

I am their blood of life made visible
I hold their part of life that vanishes.
They whisper to me, names and messages,
Lost in the world, a sifting down of shadows.

I am myself, I say, it is my blood,
It is my time of sun and lifting of green,
Nothing is here, but what I touch and see.
They cry out *we are here in the root and tree.*
It is my night, I say—and yours for sleeping.
They move their wings, I think I hear them weeping.
Blest spirits, let me be.

ANN STANFORD

AS IT IS

Wife love, father love, love of an old dog,
whatever love it is—if it is love—
is twined through stress
(disease, a wound, a blinding debt)
into so tight a skein
the leanest filament seems gross:
    threads in light bulbs,
    split ends of human hair,
    or the close, red conduits
    through which blood creaks and booms
    in echo chambers of motels,
    deserted chairs, black trains,
    or just a dusty seashell, in a drawer,
    curved like a porcelain ear.

Things shake and sigh with it—
roofs, knobs, and doors—
and common neighbors coming home,
seeing an ambulance,
a wandering, wondering child,
a foreign license plate,
an empty yard,
or furniture stacked outside
like varnished bones.

It toils and sleeps;
it wrestles and cooks meals,
copes with mountains, dust cloths, tears;
carries out trash, seeks interviews,
limps through heat; scrubs, burrows, cries,
boils water, holds a dying paw,

    does what it does
    to keep pain back awhile—if it is pain—
    as it must be
    if it is love.

ADRIEN STOUTENBURG

PENELOPE

Exhausted summer. New sails in the roadsteads are
the flags of homelessness: like you, a hearth.

Like you, I say. In the cool great rooms where dawn
unclouds as from a metal cup just emptied

and in the warm peach-coloured rooms by lamplight
I say: "Like you. Thus—thus—she was like you."

Where have been all my sailings, all my islands,
but here, by you, in search of you, my island,

whose pools, palms, dunes I feigned to find in others,
not doubting those dissembled, I dissembled.

Till, in dawn rooms, by evenings under lamplight,
turning, I find you: all my quest, and yet

(changed by my searching, borrowing from those others)
more than I left; not less than both our lives.

Exhausted summer. Removed, immortal spring.
Now go. I go, you would have me go: recalling

love that was always building, and time reframing,
a changeless spring new-made in the first spring's room.

The sailmakers whistle, they work at the flags of famine.
I sail for earth's end, where you wait, in immortal spring.

RANDOLPH STOW

FROM A LITANY

There is an open field I lie down in a hole I once dug
    and I praise the sky.
I praise the clouds that are like lungs of light.
I praise the owl that wants to inhabit me and the hawk
    that does not.
I praise the mouse's fury, the wolf's consideration.
I praise the dog that lives in the household of people
    and shall never be one of them.
I praise the whale that lives under the cold blankets of salt.
I praise the formations of squid, the domes of meandra.
I praise the secrecy of doors, the openness of windows.
I praise the depth of closets.
I praise the wind, the rising generations of air.
I praise the trees on whose branches shall sit the Cock
    of Portugal and the Polish Cock.
I praise the palm trees of Rio and those that shall grow
    in London.
I praise the gardeners, the worms and the small plants that
    praise each other.
I praise the sweet berries of Georgetown, Maine, and the song
    of the white-throated sparrow.
I praise the poets of Waverly Place and Eleventh Street,
    and the one whose bones turn to dark emeralds when he
    stands upright in the wind.
I praise the clocks for which I grow old in a day and young
    in a day.
I praise all manner of shade, that which I see and that
    which I do not.
I praise all roofs from the watery roof of the pond to the
    slate roof of the customs house.
I praise those who have made of their bodies final embassies
    of flesh.
I praise the failure of those with ambition, the authors of
    leaflets and notebooks of nothing.
I praise the moon for suffering men.
I praise the sun its tributes.

I praise the pain of revival and the bliss of decline.
I praise all for nothing because there is no price.
I praise myself for the way I have with a shovel and I
    praise the shovel.
I praise the motive of praise by which I shall be reborn.
I praise the morning whose sun is upon me.
I praise the evening whose son I am.

MARK STRAND

THE SLEEP

There is the sleep of my tongue
speaking a language I can never remember—
words that enter the sleep of words
once they are spoken.

There is the sleep of one moment
inside of the next, lengthening the night,
and the sleep of the window
turning the tall sleep of trees into glass.

The sleep of novels as they are read is soundless
like the sleep of dresses on the warm bodies of women.
And the sleep of thunder gathering dust on sunny days
and the sleep of ashes long after.

The sleep of wind has been known to fill the sky.
The long sleep of air locked in the lungs of the dead.
The sleep of a room with someone inside it.
Even the wooden sleep of the moon is possible.

And there is the sleep that demands I lie down
and be fitted to the dark that comes upon me
like another skin in which I shall never be found,
out of which I shall never appear.

MARK STRAND

THE DEATH OF A PHOTOGRAPHER

Light was his paradigm;
he wove it, a cat's cradle
to knot them in, eyes rounded
to the dead instant on paper—
an 8x10 moment—glossy.

It was a trade of stealth,
the black box a trap
for the unstilted gesture;
and maybe that is why
he stole things—

ashtrays, wives and bibles—
always in need of basics.
He had compassion for the unpossessed
objects scarred by the anonymity
of hotel rooms, never taking the new,
only those roughed with use like
the corroded edge of his pant cuff.

And the wives:
perhaps it was the stealth and
the way he saw them in secret
under the catafalque of the camera's cloth,
smiles buried upside down on

ground glass, a mask reversed;
and still their skirts were neat—
defying gravity. Like a Japanese
who had saved a life, having seen
them exposed, he felt responsible.

Late at night, after
they had left, he enlarged their faces
and watched them bloom blank paper,
a monochrome resolve, swimming from

alkali to acid. He hung them on a
clothesline and left the room
ambushed by drying smiles.

There were six wet handkerchiefs
and one dry that would not
cry here, in the cold silence
of folding chairs.
The blurred faces turned

to the clattering edge of sunlight
and walked into their own focus,
while his portrait,
in a blue blazer, was nailed
down to its dark frame.

KAREN SWENSON

ROTC: *US55415237 PASSES BY*

Out of sight down the curve of the green campus
I hear the rattle of all the bolts going back as one—
After all these years, still familiar as the sound of my breath,
This noise of boys playing at murder as if it were a minuet,
Hefting the M-1 and slapping the operating rod handle back
As if they were masters of silence.
Our tools make us.
The brute brown length of my rifle oppresses me,
And how I served it with patches and rod,
And then I think of St. Francis saying Brother Fire.
No. In spite of these boys ranked like toy soldiers,
In spite of the unjust war that they all hope to escape,
The rifle grows out of my hand.

I cross the street and think I have left the ranks behind,
But under the war-memorial, the list of the college's forgotten dead
Remembered in marble over which some subversive hand has scrawled
The round rune of peace, under the tall white trunk of iron
On which the flag flowers, they are grading a student on manual of arms.
Right Shoulder Arms.
In the center of the sidewalk, in the ring of authority,
The sergeant in khaki, the officers in green,
He moves like a puppet according to their demands
While the wide blue eye of peace watches from the dead marble
And I go by, cutting across the grass,
Unwilling to distract the professionals at their trade.

They think they can make the rifle obey with these manners
But when the long killing comes they will know better;
The mild blue hieroglyph
And the weight of the weapon balance each other
As I go across the green surface of the day.

JOHN TAYLOR

MY BOOK

This death inside, my skeleton,
paces the length of days, winter
and summer, blind. It hears nothing.
It comes no nearer taste than teeth
packed in ruts of jaw. Odors
of buildings, meadows, streets, bypass
the insensible rods of bone I carry,
that carry me.

                How shall I touch them?

Wherever I go on earth or water
or on bridges thrust over water, or higher
than that, in planes, or beneath the broad
surface of things, in caves or subways,
what is outside reaches and fills
the cavities of my body, space
of all the passages of ear,
warm places where my breath rises
and falls, all soft hollows of love
or waste or sense.

                My darkest parts,
hollows invaded every time
and way I turn with different air
keep their own secrets, are not mine,
are a new mystery, puzzling each breath
I take. Nothing I learn or love
is mine.

        The only parts that live
finally are the unknowing bones,
the anonymous spaces they define,
and this.

        Read it.

At dead center,
to which my body hurries, bone
grins with a grave rhetoric, and waits.

PHYLLIS THOMPSON

TRANSPLANT

i
'you!' I said
'what are you doing
dressed up like that?'

you in your white coat
and I like a book
in your hand

you a young white nun
in your cloister
winona   the river
reading
these images

down the snowy hallways
through lecture rooms
past beds with tubes
like long supple vines
baltimore   1961
the eye hospital

everything
like lightning
frozen into the trees

down the snowy hallways
into an old poem
about exiles

ii
later
in a dream
I returned

like a man
walking lost
in a snowy field

the surgeon
bending over
deft strokes
glint of steel

'there' he said
'all done'
and stood straight up
like an angel
his hands free now
trembling like grass
in a fresh wind

'there' he said
'come have a look
at yourself'

and I did
through the red
blurred pain of it
like a rose
and its thorn
or a hummingbird
in the song of its wings

and I saw
in the high mirror
above me
a single burned eye
in a field of snow

iii

and then you   lady
broke out of memory

like a flower
between two acts
in a crowded place

and my eyes
lived there a moment
like two flames
before you closed them

and I could see
through your face
like a stained window
in the chapel of that moment
that grew between us

the rain driven
into the dry prairies
and moving the rivers
again

and the distant lightning
at play among the trees

and the glittering
birds

and we swaying in the song
of the first wind
like two dark enormous
sunflowers

C. W. TRUESDALE

GIVING IT A NAME

Because it had beeped away night after night,
We all went out to the woods and hunted it.
A few brought flashlights and compasses to get
Into the spirit of the thing—even a shotgun,
Though there was nothing in the woods to be
Scared of, nothing worth killing. Chop one down
And you'll see there's nothing after you but stumps.

It wasn't our territory: five kinds of darkness
Crossed each other out from clump to hollow
Where the evergreens sank down to olive, ripe-olive,
And blank, in spite of patches of moonlight,
Blank: not something you'd care to put your foot in.

And we held still, lights out, to give it a chance.
After a minute, everywhere we looked
We saw fool's gold and phosphorescent logs,
The spittle of opossums, warts on toads,
The muzzles of cougars teething their own light,
The square dance of the blood at the backs of our eyes.

At last, it started—a noise without a name,
Not ominous or ghostly, not growing stronger,
Not gathering size as if it could take over,
But simply telling itself, announcing itself
Slowly and steadily and carefully,
Going in and out of phase with our heartbeats,
And something went wrong with us. We seemed to feel
It was now or nowhere, it was here or never.
Flashlight and shotgun cracked their sights together,
And we walked back to our houses single file,
The head-man carrying, wrapped up in a shirt,
The name of it, the bloody name of it.

DAVID WAGONER

A CELEBRATION FOR AUTUMN

Once more I welcome a purer darkness
Of evening in the hour of the year
Between summer and an end of summer,
When the soft air is songless as moss
Over the barn where the swallows are

Restless. Something has wearied the sun
To yellow the unmolested dust
On the bitter quince; something is lost
From its light, letting waxen bees drown
In their liquor of fatigue. But by last

Shadows of another season gone,
I live into beginning autumn
To see its silver, broken column
Of thready smoke ascending. Someone
Has gathered up his few leaves fallen

On the morning's webby lawn, who knows
Nothing of how I share them. I think
Of his hands at the live fire, and thank
Him in his private wood for what grows
Commonly for us toward the stars

I recognize of winter to come.
And I remember an August once,
With armfuls of slushing leaves, left since
Noon to dry by the hedge they fell from,
Shiny as the shears. Could we burn them

Now, I wheedled my grandfather, now?
Everything in its own due time,
He said, for fires need cold and autumn
Dark if you want their flowers to grow;
And who was I to call down the snow

Before its proper season? The weeks
Frittered on beyond the old man's dying,
And the ready pears, and my crying
In his garden rows of empty sticks.
His fire shot higher than hollyhocks

One night when the smell of dead summer
Was too much to bear. It was for me,
Who had had hardly a breath easy
From the heavy hammer of asthma,
That frost assembled in that glimmer

Of thrown smoke, and prized into my blood
Like the feel of knives over the skin.
I lived on, into its cold. Again
I tread through a crisping grass; the hard
Air closes again, and I am glad.

Some troubled sleep it may take to bear
The slump of one less summer—but clean
The sun tomorrow, or the frail rain.
I shall breathe in refreshed September.
I have much to thank my autumns for.

TED WALKER

A LOSS OF PLAYERS, ON TOUR BY FLIGHT

Before the plane came down in the moonlight like steeples,
The white wings blobbed off on the snow of the fields
A quarter-mile either side; and the held breaths
In the falling bodies must have spun out their fall
Until the fuselage meteored belly-up into this mesa.
With that it went into the world of no color
And the hushes of winter resumed.
All week after, the snowfalls continued:
And no aerial photograph taken materializes its presence;
Only by night it comes to life, privately
Printing shadows like the negative of its own picture.
The attitude of the players is fixed:
In their last exitings from blithe impostures
They lie apart stiff and square as bales of hay
Provided to the ranging cattle;
The interior wires of these bales are broken
With some spill of silage; but the snow makes no matter
Of spills; those with faces and eyes looked upward
For hours, like trout hung in water, but the snow
Makes no matter of eyes.
Something snowshoed here, something rabbited,
Something visited on a spread of wings,
Something will come again in the season of colors,
If the earth ungums; the quicksilver plane,
Cooled from molten, waits where it cratered;
And the players, drifting no great distance
Up moonstream, and downstage returning, wait.

NANCY G. WESTERFIELD

RUNICS: FOR THE EVE OF ALL HALLOWS, IN
MINSTRELSY, KENTUCKY

The road to Alexandria bands this way,
Through bluegrass hills and dairy dells;
The village founded in one faith and milking operation
Stands a stitch of houses to its seam of road;
New road gap-proof, plumb-driven;
Old road a cratered footway paved with grasses
Up from the riffled waterbed; both roads climb
To Corpus Christi church and yard.
The graves lean downhill toward the town;
The village and the outdoor shrines lean hillward;
The road to Alexandria bands this way, and away again.

I band this way,
Once in the company of one, and now alone;
One in Minstrelsy created himself in his own image,
From Minstrelsy came forth and barded the world
With Sodom songs, all of them Minstrelsy;
But he said: it was Deadsville he left behind him,
And a cold journey afoot through the traitored roadway,
Trestle-walking the gap-toothed ridges to freedom:
You would have thought it the least place for song.
But he was full of it, grace of beginnings,
And he had all of us singing,
Until with pride Minstrelsy saw him buried
In Corpus Christi yard, and with pride sees him visited.

In that talismaned town tonight
The doorstoops burn pumpkin-heads;
This people-patch burns too, with moonlight:
The moon in a mask inserting itself into the hedge
Picks at the cuneiform stones, picks locks of the dead;
The graveboxes tumble downhill under the ground
To sewage the town; salt-white the crumbling headstones
Nimble it downhill to rendezvous with the town;
The skulls ripening in the vines of their vertebrae,

Biting the earth with once-familiar faces,
Are all umbilicaled to the town.
"Turn back, turn back, and you pillar to salt," he said;
But I who loved you better than salt
Bid you rise tonight, put on your death's head,
Walk in that clutch of houses spawning the indoor souls,
Pilfer the life the livers there save up for living.
"Who saves life to be lived in tomorrows?"
Once you said, your mouth mouthing mine,
"I'll take his life." And all of the life
That Minstrelsy's dead had saved for a century
Exploded itself in you,
And still goes on explosive.

"Bake me a troll-cake," you said,
"And I'll dance to your hours";
O dance me again tonight, on a nip of life,
The suite of our quarrels,
Where you brought all the arts to bear on me:
How as chorales you first built their beginnings:
Your antiphoned phrases and mine
Fell out with each other like hymns talking,
Until your allemande of a reprimand,
And the dizzied bourrées than spun after;
How in the postures of anger
You struck all the classic positions,
To my own grim arms and grimaces,
Till the grace of your grammar at dancing à deux
Furied me out of all syntax;
O dance me to crumbs again at the feet of your table!
In the gigue of your hot death take me your partner.

Pell-mell, pell-mell, the bell-pull jibes
With our pulled bells; we are all pendulums;
Living and dead, we are all swung
From Corpus Christi clock, all hung from Minstrelsy's bell;
The bare warp of winter elms webs with the morning stars;
The morning wind shakes the facade in the rose-windowed church;
The school-windows shine with up-rumped cats

And the faggots for witches; morning annuls
Those last pillagers loose in the unbewitched town;
The skulls without lights writhing back on umbilicals
Turn crooknecks like squashes,
Knuckle under and burrow the knoll.
In the rot and rotation of things
Doorstep milks curdle,
Pumpkin-heads swelling to rot drop orange teeth,
The life goes out of our thimblesful;
And your paper mouth under the mask turns to dead again
As you turn to look back at me,
With uncandled eyes, all the yolk spilled out of your shell.
Still Minstrelsy's hope of an immortality engenders your own:
The road to Alexandria springs signs of your birthplace;
This gate springs with word of your whereabouts
Sleeping to Minstrelsy's waking; after the terror
Of so many days of your walking, the town wakes
To pillar you preserved for its glory;
And my own hope of your immortality that speeched you here
In my empty embracing, engenders your last laughter:
When in the afterglow of your hot death,
The phosphorus flare of your mind's sight
Briefly encompassing all,
All our afterlife hoped-for you entered and spent
To your own satisfied incandescence.

In the rot and rotation of things
I have left you there; but I say
Your poems like prayers; your best lines
Still spit in the mouth like salted sunflower seeds.

NANCY G. WESTERFIELD

SUGAR DADDY

To my daughter aged one

You do not look like me. I'm glad
England failed to colonise
Those black orchid eyes
With blue, the colour of sun-blindness.

Your eyes came straight to you
From your mother's Martinique
Great-grandmother. They look at me
Across this wide Atlantic

With an inborn feeling for my weaknesses.
Like love-letters, your little phoney grins
Come always just too late
To reward my passionate clowning.

I am here to be nice, clap hands, reflect
Your tolerance. I know what I'm for.
When you come home fifteen years from now
Saying you've smashed my car,

I'll feel the same. I'm blood-brother,
Sugar-daddy, millionaire to you.
I want to buy you things.

I bought a garish humming top
And climbed into your pen like an ape
And pumped it till it screeched for you,
Hungry for thanks. Your lip

Trembled and you cried. You did not need
My sinister grenade, something
Pushed out of focus at you, swaying
Violently. You owned it anyway

And the whole world it came from.
It was then I knew
I could only take things from you from now on.

I was the White Hunter
Bearing cheap mirrors for the chief.
You saw the giving-look coagulate in my eyes
And panicked for the trees.

HUGO WILLIAMS

THE DAY ZIMMER LOST RELIGION

The first Sunday I missed Mass on purpose
I waited all day for Christ to climb down
Like a wiry flyweight from the cross and
Club me on my irreverent teeth, to wade into
My blasphemous gut and drop me like a
Red hot thurible, the devil roaring in
Reserved seats until he got the hiccups.

It was a long cold way from the old days
When cassocked and surpliced I mumbled Latin
At the old priest and rang his obscure bell.
A long way from the dirty wind that blew
The soot like venial sins across the school yard
Where God reigned as a threatening,
One-eyed triangle high in the fleecy sky.

The first Sunday I missed Mass on purpose
I waited all day for Christ to climb down
Like the playground bully, the cuts and mice
Upon his face agleam, and pound me
Till my irreligious tongue hung out.
But of course He never came, knowing that
I was grown up and ready for Him now.

PAUL ZIMMER